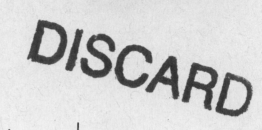
P9-DFL-038

DISCARD

miraculous
silence

DISCARD

miraculous silence

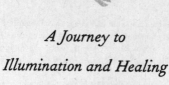

A Journey to
Illumination and Healing
Through Prayer

mitra rahbar

EDITED BY MINOO RAHBAR

ILLUSTRATIONS BY LAUREN SEBASTIAN

JEREMY P. TARCHER/PENGUIN
an imprint of Penguin Random House
New York

JEREMY P. TARCHER/PENGUIN
An imprint of Penguin Random House LLC
375 Hudson Street
New York, New York 10014

Copyright © 2015 by Mitra Rahbar
Penguin supports copyright. Copyright fuels creativity, encourages diverse voices,
promotes free speech, and creates a vibrant culture. Thank you for buying an
authorized edition of this book and for complying with copyright laws by not
reproducing, scanning, or distributing any part of it in any form without permission.
You are supporting writers and allowing Penguin to continue to
publish books for every reader.

Most Tarcher/Penguin books are available at special quantity discounts for bulk
purchase for sales promotions, premiums, fund-raising, and educational needs.
Special books or book excerpts also can be created to fit specific needs.
For details, write: SpecialMarkets@penguinrandomhouse.com.

Library of Congress Cataloging-in-Publication Data

Names: Rahbar, Mitra.
Title: Miraculous silence : a journey to illumination and healing through prayer /
Mitra Rahbar ; illustrations by Lauren Sebastian.
Description: New York : Jeremy P. Tarcher-Penguin, 2015. | Includes bibliographical
references and index.
Identifiers: LCCN 2015040085 | ISBN 978-0-399-17550-3
Subjects: LCSH: Spiritual life. | Prayer. | Meditation. | Spiritual healing. | Mental
healing. | Precious stones—Miscellanea.
Classification: LCC BL624 .R3235 2015 | DDC 204/.3—dc23 LC record available at
https://protect-us.mimecast.com/s/nKX5BnSzmpA4F0

Printed in the United States of America
1   3   5   7   9   10   8   6   4   2

Book design by Marysarah Quinn

Neither the publisher nor the author is engaged in rendering professional advice or services
to the individual reader. The ideas, procedures, and suggestions contained in this book
are not intended as a substitute for consulting with your physician. All matters regarding
your health require medical supervision. Neither the author nor the publisher shall be
liable or responsible for any loss or damage allegedly arising from any information or
suggestion in this book.

If you wish for Light, be ready to receive Light.

—RUMI

In honor of all the spirits who have guided me . . .

I dedicate this book to the spirits
of my precious Khale and my beloved Baba.
I know you were with me
as I embarked on this journey of devotion.
Through each passage and prayer,
you were always there.

I love you . . .

You are my forever treasure.

table of contents

prayers

PRAYERS FOR HEALING

PRAYERS FOR ILLNESS AND LOSS

PRAYERS FOR SPECIAL OCCASIONS

frequently asked questions and references

preface

From the time I found myself and my voice, I knew and felt my connection to the Divine. I knew God before I could speak— maybe not the word, but I knew God in the very fiber of my being; I knew I had come here with this faith and knowledge. At barely the age of four, in a conversation with my mother, I asked, "Did God create us all?"

"Yes," my mother replied.

"Then we all have to love each other, because we're made by the same God," I said. In that moment, I felt the birth of a greater love in me: God resided in each of us, and therefore we were all connected. We were all the children of God. The seed of my soul had awakened to this knowledge that our Eternal Parent is the sacred thread that weaves us all together in this tapestry of life.

As a young child, this understanding, coupled with my outgoing personality, led me to embrace everyone with a smile and a hug. I felt a knowing comfort in this connection. Strangers at first appeared to hesitate when I would smile at them, but in a matter of moments, each heart would melt at the sight of a young child who would not stop smiling. In a split second, my smile would be reciprocated!

As a teenager, I found myself in a new country—due to political unrest in my homeland—far removed from all I knew, loved, and understood. The trials of immigration, loss of loved ones, financial struggles, and my deep longing for my beloved homeland and family were depleting the reserves of my young life. With the passage of time, my inner baggage was getting heavier. I found refuge in prayer circles comprised of women only. There, in the hours of chanting, and amidst the cries of my many sisters, I would lose myself in the infinite love of the Divine. As a young woman, pregnant tears would burst fervently upon my face, awakening a deep longing that would call to me. The prayers and chants were a much needed quiet for my yearning soul, but deep in my core, I knew that soon I would be unable to withstand the weight of the heavy baggage that remained with me.

The suicide of a dear friend led me to the altar of a sacred sanctuary one afternoon in the midst of winter. My body could not contain my disbelief and shock. I swayed with this grief for countless minutes. Suddenly, I felt a hand on my head. I heard a voice as I lifted my eyes.

"You have cried enough. God has heard you," said an elderly man with a captivating presence. "Get up," he said. I got up, in a haze, taken by his commanding demeanor and gentle voice.

In the months that followed, the whimper of my soul was slowly becoming a cry, screaming, "Look at me, *look at me*." A choice was upon me: to look or to ignore. The words of the old man kept ringing in my ears. Until that moment, I had understood prayer as going to a place of worship or just talking to God and allowing my soul to be dissolved in the Infinite. But this stranger had proposed a new thought to me: *God had heard me. I had been heard*. These four words opened the pathways of my mind to a deeper understanding of prayer and my connection to God. They implied that I could have a conversation with God, that He was within my reach, not somewhere far, but *here* with me. With that, I decided. I looked. I devoted myself to creating sacred space each day and laid my tired body at the gates of God's love. I chanted, meditated, visualized, used stones, prayed . . . and prayed.

In those years, in the midst of my inner chaos, I chose to delve deeper into my soul, peeling aside the layers of pain, one by one, to create healing. Like a soldier on a mission, I devoted my life to this. I would sit with God, talk with God, and rest with God. As I slowly unraveled, I could see a radiant light at my core—one that was fearless, with beautiful brilliance, as designed by the Beloved. The prayers had taken me to the seed of my soul, beyond the chatter and clutter. I could barely contain myself as my tears would birth a joy and love so profound upon my chest and being. In this silence, I had found the most precious and treasured gift of all: *God and me*.

When friends would invite me out, I would leave early, thinking, I have a date with God! Sitting in prayer was the best part of my day . . . and of me. He was always waiting, and I was always yearning.

For my entire life up to that point, I had been swimming against the tides of my culture, my peers, my friends, and my age. This had created some inner conflict and discomfort in me, although I had always followed my truth and heard my voice clearly. As I emerged, so did another truth: I realized that the tides were *my* tides, and I was following my own current; I embraced being different and choosing differently. In this acceptance and honoring of the self, I broke through the walls of judgment, guilt, and self-pity and found a new freedom of self and life. I surrendered to the divine design of the Universe and all its splendor.

In over three decades of work, I have seen the yearning and emptiness we can all experience. I have seen the waves of uncertainty and fear that can wash out our reserve. And I have seen and known that our only real anchor is faith. It is faith that keeps us from staying down. It is faith that lifts us when we cannot find the strength to stand. And it is faith that sits in the space between the fall and the standing.

To me, prayer was and is the best part of me, my life, and my day. I have never known another way but prayer—to awaken the heart and find the deep, loving bond with its Maker. As faith fuels me, anchors me, and guides me, *prayer* quiets me and connects me more deeply and beautifully to God. In the sacred space of prayer, there is no hierarchy and there are no separations: there is only the child and the Maker. None of His children is more valued, none more precious; all are equally loved, each special and beautiful to the Eternal Parent; there is only unconditional love.

As the prayers found me, and I them, I realized that my life and my breath were a prayer each day. Today I know no other way of facing the travesties or unfairness we all sometimes witness or experience. As I know the sun shall rise tomorrow, I know what our planet needs for its healing is prayer—for prayer is the portal to the goodness, the light, that resides within us. This is the light that will lead us to a world and life of nonviolence, of harmony, compassion, kindness, and ultimately, peace.

As this little book of prayer is now finished, I already miss the journey it took me on—a magical ride into the heart of the Beloved, sealed forever within my soul.

My hope is that this collection of prayers will be a gateway to healing and a portal to self-love and God's love. As you receive these prayers with your heart, may you further create healing in your life and the world.

With love, I offer you these prayers—these passages to enlightenment, devotion, and healing. As you open your hearts to them, may you feel that the hand of God is lifting you, even when you cannot see it. As you read, may you believe, and as you believe, may you connect to the brilliance and beauty that lies between your heart and God.

I offer you *Miraculous Silence*.

notes from the author

My hope is that *Miraculous Silence* will be received as intended—a book of prayers for healing and illumination for all. Here are a few notes, distinctions, and suggestions that I hope will enhance your experience and bring more clarity to the book's contents:

- The words chosen to refer to God in this book are not meant to reflect any specific religion, but to allow for interpretation by the reader based on his or her own religious or spiritual background and/or to reflect the popular understanding of universal spirit/energy/source.
- Many titles are used interchangeably in referring to God— for example, Lord, Father, Mother, Eternal Parent, Beloved, Spirit, Divine, Light, Source, Maker.
- For consistency and simplicity, the masculine pronoun "He" is often used in reference to God, but it can be replaced with "She" based on the belief system or preference of the reader.
- Mother Earth is used to refer to the energy—the spirit of the earth—that nurtures us all.
- The words "Kingdom," "Creation," and "Universe" here are meant as a nonreligious reference to *all of creation*—the space of God's domain.
- The words "Amen," *Namaste* (Sanskrit, "I bow to you"), *Khodaya* (Farsi, "oh God," to call to the Divine), and *Shokran* (Arabic, "to give thanks") are used as ending notes for certain prayers throughout the book. Their derivation from different backgrounds reflects the book's universal outlook.

- For best results, please release any judgments that might arise regarding body posture or specific mind-sets during the practices recommended here (meditation, mantra, etc.). Allow the practice to take its own form. Let your body and higher intuition guide you.
- The essence of any type of spiritual practice is intention. When the intention of the soul is to bring forth healing and awareness, all the pieces fall into place and flow beautifully. Intention, along with discipline, patience, belief, and allowance (openness of the mind and heart), are key to a fulfilling practice.
- Many prayers in the book include suggestions for the use of stones or mantras. These suggestions are meant to further enhance your healing and bring greater illumination to the focus of the prayer, but are completely optional. Integrate any of these suggestions only if you feel moved to, noting that while many choices are given, using just one or two stones and/or mantras is sufficient.
- Vedic and Buddhist mantras are used frequently in the prayers because these traditions have the largest collections of mantras.
- During any of the prayers and/or sacred space practices in this book, a white candle can be lit to provide further support in becoming focused and centered. The candle is not only comforting but also enhances our space. When praying for someone other than yourself, you may light additional candles.
- It is recommended that you remove jewelry (unless it has a special significance to you) and turn off mobile phones and other potential distractions during any of these sacred space practices. You might also run your hands through cold water to neutralize your energy fields.

opening prayer

Prayer is a whisper of the soul.
Prayer is a yearning of the heart.
Prayer is a nakedness of being,
in receiving God.

Let your soul sing this song.
Let your heart beat with this pulse.
Let your body let go
and be with the Light,
as intended.

Speak, sing, be silent . . .
Just open your soul to *you*.
Open your soul to the Infinite . . .
There,
lies only a place of peace,
a place of love.

When this love is upon you,
when your pregnant tears give birth to release,
when laughter fills each cell of your body with love,
when your sigh becomes a connection
with everything around you . . .
this will be Grace,

upon each strand,
each note,
each pause.

You will be in the highest joy,
in the most poignant moment,
in the most profound comfort . . .
You will be with God.

Allow this,
create this,
and become this:
a light bearer
of the Divine.

sacred space
(introduction)

From a very young age, we learn to create space for all we do. We initially learn this from our bodies, instinctively, as we tune into our inner rhythms and, for example, know when we are hungry, and when we need to sleep. As we get older, we create other external spaces for playing, resting, eating, and doing homework. In time, we create physical space for our books, clothes, furniture, and electronics, and time slots for all the important activities of the day. We learn to value and respect these spaces and activities, and they become the fabric of our daily existence.

Soon, however, the life we have created is governed by these allowances. All the available physical space for our possessions, and time slots on the daily "to-do" list, become very congested. And now in the age of modern technology, it has become commonplace for us to fill whatever remaining space we might have with a barrage of "virtual" interactions, such as social media and texting, until there is simply no space left at all.

As a result, we may feel a sense of deep discontent over time, a void beyond what we can even express. Although our lives appear to be so full of activity, so filled with possessions, we may feel restless, anxious, or profoundly unfulfilled. This is the emptiness that results when the heart is void of devotion, of being with God. When we allow ourselves an instant of true quiet, we might hear a whisper or, at times, a powerful cry. This is our soul yearning for the Divine, reminding us that we have a task at hand; no one can ignore this cry for too long, for the anguish and decay will grow deeper and deeper.

The inner child longs for the embrace and caress of the Eternal Parent—the Beloved—and it is only in this connection that the soul can regain its peace. The umbilical cord linking soul to God is never cut, even as our preoccupation with the physical realm and its ceaseless activity seems to take priority.

The irony of this no-more-space/no-more-time reality is this: we have ignored the most important, fulfilling, and life-altering space there is—sacred space. *Miraculous Silence* is largely about reclaiming this space of worship, of light, of devotion, of connection with the Divine, through prayer and other supportive practices. This is, in fact, the only space we really have that consistently fuels us on the deepest level and provides us with true joy, happiness, and peace.

We create this sacred space physically, spiritually, emotionally, and mentally within our core. As we open our hearts and awaken to the light that governs the Universe, we connect to the light within our own being. We create a sacred space to sit, talk, and be with God. We may have faith and feel like we know God, but now we recognize that to be at peace, to be fulfilled, to be elevated, and to be enlightened, we must not only believe but also engage in a devotional practice of connecting more deeply with God.

Imagine a beautiful garden, lush with vibrant colors and alive with rich fragrance. We find a space of green grass amidst it, take off our shoes, and sit or lie down and embrace the warmth of the earth. Once we do, we are able to take in the beauty of the garden and bask in the full glory of the sun. Similarly, we need to create the sacred space within by tapping gently on the door of the soul. As it opens, we will see an even more magnificent garden—a feast for our senses—as we bask in the glory of God.

The door to the spiritual garden of the soul can be opened through prayer and practices such as meditation, visualization, and reciting mantras. Devotion to such disciplines will open this sacred space beautifully.

> *Wherever you are in your journey, I invite you to*
> *create this space, to allow it, and to embrace it. What*
> *will unfold to you will be a sacred space of ultimate*
> *peace—the ultimate gift you can receive . . .*
> *a miraculous silence.*

understanding prayer

*As food is necessary for the body, prayer
is necessary for the soul . . . believing in
God, man cannot, should not live a
moment without prayer.*

—MAHATMA GANDHI

Prayer is an integral part of devotion. Understanding the significance and meaning of prayer will allow us to access a deeper place of intention and allowance while praying.

WHAT IS PRAYER?

Prayer is sitting with God and opening our hearts to Him. It is the act of communion with God. It is a calling out to God, optimally from a pure place within our soul, from the light within. It is a pure intention of the heart to be with the Divine. Whether in silence, or in the form of a whisper, a cry, a spoken word, a song, or a movement, the essence is the same: prayer is always between you and God.

WHAT ARE THE ORIGINS OF PRAYER?

The origins of prayer are unknown. However, we can only assume that from the time humans have existed on Earth, prayer has also existed in some form—be it as a conversation, a silence, or any other form of communication from the heart. There may not have been words that defined God or prayer, but in the depth of each heart there must have always been a connection, a communication to Source, that perhaps could not be named or defined.

WHY IS PRAYER IMPORTANT?

One of the best ways to reach true spiritual enlightenment is through prayer. Prayer is as critical to our spiritual being as water and food are to our physical bodies. A body that is malnourished will be more susceptible to illness. Similarly, a soul that does not communicate, or sit, with God may feel more restless or incomplete.

The cry of a baby can only be quieted by the tender touch of a mother's love. We are each the child, and God is our Mother, our Father. The child needs to be held in the embrace of the Eternal Parent. We need to allow ourselves to be embraced by, and in, this divine love. One of the best ways to achieve this is through prayer.

When we pray, we allow ourselves to become whole, at peace, ignited by the love of the Divine, better understanding not only the realms of existence but also the connection of all forms of life and spirit to one another.

Find a physical space you are comfortable with and allow yourself to go to the deepest, purest place within your soul. Allow yourself to open your heart to the Divine. Do not focus on the words but on your heart: what does it wish to express? Close your eyes and reconnect to your inner core. You may not find words, but if you allow yourself to just be and feel, you will connect to the depth of your emotions, and they will flow and channel through you. As you relax more into this and allow yourself to sit nakedly before God, you will unveil yourself to God, and come closer to your truth. This is your communion, and in these moments your heart is connecting with the Divine and your soul is speaking to God. You will experience moments of miraculous silence in thought, speaking, and feeling. This is prayer.

Prayer needs to come from a place of purity and goodness, void of ego or pride. If our hearts and thoughts are impure, even the most beautiful of spoken words will be meaningless. But if our hearts are calling to the Beloved from the space of our inner light, our prayers will come from a place of pure intention.

Those who pray only occasionally may need to consciously create this sacred space; however, with regular devotion to the practice of prayer, we can more easily access this space. For sages, prophets, and men and women of the cloth—who are disciplined practitioners and have incorporated prayer into each moment of their lives—the space can typically be easily accessed. As we weave prayer into our daily routines, we can also access the sacred space without much effort and without conscious thought. This is truly allowing and living with the Divine in the landscape of our daily life.

WHERE DO I PRAY?

Throughout the world, people of various religions and back-grounds have their own ways and places to practice prayer. Many go to mosques, temples, churches, or synagogues to find that sacred space of prayer, while others may pray in the private sanctuary of their home or in nature. In truth, God is within our hearts at all times. He awaits us, at any moment, at any place, to be with Him.

Prayer is about allowing and opening the sacred space within—no matter where we are. It need not be limited to places of worship but can take place anywhere—in a car in the middle of the highway, in an airplane, or in a kitchen. Many have expressed to me that they constantly speak to God while driving. Is this prayer of less value than that of a person who goes to a house of worship to pray? No, the value is in the purity of the intention behind the prayer, not the location.

WHEN DO I PRAY?

Prayer can be done at any time, in any place, at any moment. God does not ever move away from us. He is the Only Constant.

Many turn to prayer only when they feel desperate or lost, or when they want to ask for something. It is never wrong to turn to God, in any circumstance or way, but as the great poet and philosopher Khalil Gibran states, "You pray in your distress and in your need; would that you might pray also in the fullness of your joy and in your days of abundance." The heart yearns to seek God not only in times of distress but also in times of joy and confidence.

Prayer can best create enlightenment and true spiritual growth when it is interwoven with our daily life. Do we think of eating one day but not the next? Do we think of sleeping one day but not the next? No, for food and rest are integral parts of our physical well-being. And similarly, prayer is an integral part of our spiritual well-being, elevation, and inner growth. When we pray each day, we are allowing our inner soul to sit with the Light, to be nurtured, loved, and nourished. God becomes a part of us, not something we think of only once in a while when we feel desperate or lonely.

HOW DO I CHOOSE THE WORDS TO PRAY?

Sometimes words do not suffice, or we simply cannot find the words to express our hearts' prayers. At such times, just sit with God. You will find Him in your heart. He resides there. Do not analyze or overthink it. Just allow yourself to be, to unveil— therein lies your truth. As your feelings flow, the words may follow. However, remember that even if the words do not come to you, or if you cannot formulate the words well, your heart will still find God and communicate with Him. Your sentiments will ring of truth and purity.

CAN PRAYER HAVE NO WORDS?

Yes! Prayer is communion with God. Some may pray through dance, others through song, and others through their silent moments. They may feel the sacredness of their inner space and open their hearts in connecting and communicating with God without using spoken words. The soul does not need words to pray to the Divine; it only needs an open heart to embrace this communion.

IS THERE ONE FORM OF PRAYER?

No, there are many forms of prayer. The existing forms of prayer used by people throughout the world are varied and diverse, based on religion, tradition, faith, culture, and personal preference. For example, in traditional Islam the *namaz* is done five times a day, in sitting and standing positions, while in Sufism (the mystical dimension of Islam) prayer may be done through whirling, losing oneself in Infinite Grace. In Judaism, prayer may be done with shuckling (swaying of the body), while Christians may bow their heads or kneel during prayer. In Hinduism, the chanting of mantras may be used as a form of prayer, while some Native Americans may conduct prayer by dancing in rhythms.

Different people and traditions have various rituals for praying, such as washing hands, taking off shoes, or wearing a specific headdress. Some use verses or passages from a holy book, while others may speak out loud, using their own words. Some may use songs, chants, or movements, while others pray in silence and stillness. Some pray in groups, while others do so individually.

No matter the form, the essence of prayer does not change: it is to find a connection to the Divine.

WHAT ARE THE BENEFITS OF
PRAYER WITH A GROUP?

Prayer is a powerful practice—not only in bringing us closer to God, but to each other. In addition to praying individually, we can also pray with a group. When prayers are done in group settings—whether in synagogues, mosques, churches, or temples—the word "me" is often replaced by "us." This creates a communal feeling and a synergy of selflessness, of all becoming one—as links of a chain—and brings us closer together, as we share our pain, our joy, and our connection to the Divine.

Another benefit to group prayer is that we can use it as a powerful tool for praying collectively for the world, creating healing light, and bringing us closer to humanity. Together with others, we bring forth compassion and kindness, which we can carry into our daily lives and our communities. This is one of the most powerful and healing ways to pray.

ARE PRAYERS ANSWERED?

Some people practice prayer primarily because their souls crave, love, desire, and long for it, and from it, they receive their ultimate fulfillment. But many pray to God to find a solution to a dilemma or to make a specific request.

Over the years, many have expressed their frustration to me, saying that their prayers have not been heard or answered although they sat earnestly, with pure intentions, night after night. "Ask and it will be given to you," states Matthew 7:7, so when people do not receive what they have asked for, they feel disheartened. However, the next verse in Matthew holds the answer: "Search, and you will find; knock, and the door will be opened to you." The key is the last few words: "the door will be opened to you." This door may be that of knowledge, of faith, grace, or wisdom. Through continued prayer, the light will be shown to us to guide our way, and we will receive our answer—even if it is different from what we had hoped and wished for.

If we feel our prayers have not been answered, we must trust and have faith that there is a divine reason—we may not be ready for it, it may not be intended by Spirit for us at this time, or it may not be part of our soul's journey. We need to honor God's plan for us. At such times, we need to learn to surrender our human wishes and expectations, and simply "give it to God."

Once you integrate prayer into the landscape of your life, you will see flowers blooming at each turn. This is prayer: the awakening of the heart to Creation.

prayers

devotional
prayers

I AM THY GOD

I am not of earth or sky.
I am not of sea or wind.
I am not of fire or rain.
I am not seen or touched.
I am not heard or silenced.

I am not of matter or structure.
I am not of form or design.
I am not fluid or solid.
I am not future or past.

I am the Creator.
I am All, and there is nothing but I.
I am that which has no definition.
I am that which is eternal.
I am the Only . . .
Timeless.
Light.
Love.

I am thy God.

THE ALWAYS CONSTANT

I am here,
the Always Constant.

I am here,
in quiet or chaos.

I am here,
in peace or turmoil.

I need no explanation.
I need not your eyes to see me
but your heart to feel me.

I need not your mind to question me,
but your soul to search for the only truth that is . . .
I am.
I am within you.
I am all that you see around you.
I am all there is—
that which you see
and that which you do not.
I am it all.

My children are of different forms and colors.
All are of me.
All are intertwined.

I am the parent,
and you are all my children.

There is no present, past, or future . . .
All is passing and fluid as time.

You all know me.
Even those who say they do not,
know me in their quiet.

Those who denounce me know me
but question my ways.

Those who pray and speak to me know me.
When they close their eyes,
they feel me.

Search not for me between walls and borders,
but in the love that is between you.
I lie there . . .

You need not understand me,
but learn to understand yourself,
and through this,
you will see me more clearly.

I am to see all.
I am to help you elevate.
I am to be your guide.
I am to be your God.

I am here.
Hear me.
Listen . . .

In the wind and rain,
breeze and hail,
cold and heat,
it is I,
caressing you always.

In my children,
Sun, Moon, and Stars,
you will find my heavenly home
nestled in the sky.

In my children,
Ocean and Earth,
you will find your comfort and sanctuary.
And in my forests and deserts,
you will seek your refuge.

Know,
in each turn,
in each quake,
in each thunder,
I am the Always Constant.

And you are forever
my child.

Here,
now,
and always.

THAT WHICH IS

That which is given,
and that which is mine to keep,
and yet never belongs to me . . .

That which is beyond me
and yet within me,
and that which resides within the core
and the entirety of my existence . . .

That which I can still see
in the deep, silent darkness
when I close my eyes . . .

That which is beyond the moon and stars,
and encompasses the mountains
and the cycles of nature . . .

That which cannot be defined
and yet,
is the definition
of all that is seen,
felt, heard, touched, or sensed . . .

That which lies within me,
and strengthens me
in the height of calamity,
so I do not collapse . . .

That which awakens within me,
when I cannot bear waking up
to face myself . . .

That which is love,
replacing all longing,
releasing all fear and anger,
all greed and guilt . . .

That which is the voice of truth,
even when I choose not to hear . . .

That which is more sacred than any flesh or blood . . .
past, present, or future . . .

That which is so much more,
and beyond my realm of thought or vision . . .

That which believes in me
even when I do not,
is kind to me
even when I am not,
and forgives me
even when I cannot . . .
Always.

That which makes sense
when I do not . . .
That which needs no explanation . . .

That
is
God.

I AM ALWAYS HERE

It is I who holds you.
It is I who lifts you.
It is I who believes in you always.
It is I who loves you from before time began.
It is I who will never leave you.

Although you forget me at times,
question me at times,
denounce me at times,
I will never stop believing in you,
I will always carry you . . .
for you are my child,
my creation.

I will never forget you.
I will never begrudge you.
I will never turn my back on you.

See me,
for I am here.
In silence and chaos,
I sit beside you.

See me,
for I am within you . . .
the Light in the darkness,
and the Light in the light.

See me,
for then you will see only
the face of Love in each turn.

And you will know . . .
I am always here.

⌒

ONCE AGAIN

Sometimes we are unable to see the light of God, for our disappointments and sorrows feel overwhelming. At such moments, simply sit with God and feel His embrace.

STONES TO USE
RHODONITE: *to center and redirect to the higher self*
TURQUOISE: *to heal and connect to Spirit*
LAPIS LAZULI: *to see through the eyes of higher wisdom*
GIRASOL: *to bring forth the inner joy of being*

MANTRA
Chant the name of the Divine, in any way that you wish

When love disappoints and friendships fail,
when life seems to go in a different direction

than what we had hoped for,
when parents die and families disperse,
when life crumbles and our dreams are shattered . . .

In the heaviness of being in such moments,
as we sit alone in darkness of thought,
unable to see the light that carries us each day . . .

In a space within our hearts,
in the core of our existence . . .

There,
sits God,
always,
awaiting us.

As we sit in this sacred space,
the rays of light become brighter and fill our hearts,
and slowly,
the clouds of gray drift away . . .

And there,
magically,
in a moment of time,
we find hope,
we find colors,
we find life.

There,
we see God.

Lifted
into a place of healing,
slowly,
we emerge . . .
whole again.

The promise of seasons,
the promise that time does not hold still,
the promise that this too shall pass,
lightens the heavy-burdened heart.

There,
we sit with God . . .
our only Ever Constant,
forever and beyond . . .
our Everything.

As we lay our head on His lap,
we sleep . . .
His embrace lifts all sorrow
from our weary soul.

With the awakening of daylight,
our eyelids open
to a brand-new day of promise.

All is possible now,
for once again,
we see God.

I COME TO YOU

At times, we need to simply sit at the doorway of the Divine and allow our soul to cry. And in this quiet, we can listen . . . and hear the whisper of Truth. Allow, and you will find your answer.

STONES TO USE

ROSE QUARTZ: *to heal, to honor the self*

RUBY/GARNET: *to create vitality, to renew the spirit*

MOSS AGATE: *to restore*

GIRASOL: *to bring forth optimism*

AMBER: *to soothe and lift the spirit*

LAPIS LAZULI: *to connect to higher wisdom*

MALACHITE/ONYX/TOPAZ: *to strengthen*

MANTRAS

"Thy love is upon me, I trust my heart will see"

SATNAM: *to connect with your higher truth*

SO HUM/HAM SA: *to connect to the breath of life and the Universe*

Mangala Charan Mantra (see appendix A)

Chant the name of the Divine, in any way that you wish

MEDITATION/VISUALIZATION

As you breathe in and out, see a beautiful golden white light within and around you. Nestle your being in this embrace. Sit with it and allow it to cradle you.

I have come to You in quiet.

I have come to You in anger.

I have come to You screaming.

I have come to You not understanding.

I have always come to You.

I understand not the twists and turns my life has taken.
I understand not why the castle of my dreams
crumbled so quickly before my eyes.
I understand not the bleeding of my torn heart,
through dark nights of sheer terror.
I understand not.

I ask You today to lift me,
for my legs are weak and cannot carry me.
I ask You to help me build a new castle of dreams.
I ask You to guide me,
so I can make sense of the senselessness.
And, above all,
I ask You to bring vibrant colors
into the dullness of my world.

Let my heart sing of joy, of pride.
Let my eyes light up with the promise of a new day.
Let me feel whole again,
so I can be all I was intended to be.

This is my deepest prayer,
as I lay myself
at Your door.
Khodaya,*
please receive me.

Shokran[†]

---

* "Oh Divine," or "Oh God"
† Arabic word meaning "to give thanks"

TO SERVE GOD

STONE TO USE

LAPIS LAZULI: *to connect to higher truth and wisdom*

MANTRAS

"Guide me to serve"

"I am the breath of Love"

"I am a light of Light"

"Thy love is the light I carry"

"I bow to Your grace"

SO HUM / HAM SA: *to connect to the breath of life and the Universe*

SATNAM: *to connect to our higher truth*

Chant the name of the Divine, in any way that you wish

Dear God,
I have always sought You.

I have prayed each day and night
to serve You,
to be an instrument of Your divine work . . .
an instrument like the lute,*
each string creating a resonance,
a sound,
of Your divine ways.

I am an eternal student of Your light.
I am a student learning each day,
hoping to see You more clearly
with my heart,

---

* A plucked stringed instrument

hoping to understand the complexities
of Your divine tapestry . . .
complex,
yet oh, so simple.

Through each breath,
I pray to purify my soul,
to sit with my higher self,
to find deeper connection with You.

I pray to live each day
in divine light and grace,

through my actions, deeds, and thoughts,
and to lay to rest each night
in clear conscience,
knowing I have served You,
and made a difference here,
on Earth.

Dear God,
as the lute, the harp,
the song that rejoices in Your name,
I wish to create vibrations
of peace,
of love,
of Eternal Light . . .

I have no greater wish,
no higher ambition,
than to serve You.

This is my deepest,
most profound prayer.

Shokran

MEDITATION CIRCLE CHANT

In various cultures, religions, and spiritual practices, people come together to pray and chant in unison. This becomes a powerful experience that helps many enter a trancelike state of meditation and devotion. This meditative prayer can be chanted by groups of two or more, and can be repeated in various rhythms. Dim or turn off the lights; as you sit in silence, slowly, softly recite or chant this prayer, and let your heart and voice become one.

MANTRA
Use passages from this prayer as a mantra. This can be done in rhythmic patterns as you choose.

In each breath . . . it is You.
In each turn . . . it is You.
In the quiet of the night . . . it is You.
In the break of dawn . . . it is You.
In the midst of beauty . . . it is You.
In each particle of nature . . . it is You.
In times of deep love and hope . . . it is You.
In sickness and suffering . . . it is You.
In health and joy . . . it is You.
In weakness and fragility . . . it is You.
In patience and strength . . . it is You.
In laughter and tears . . . it is You.
In emptiness and fulfillment . . . it is You.
In prayer and devotion . . . it is You.
In life and rebirth . . . it is You.
In each breath . . . it is You.

It is always You,
the One I turn to,
the only One I am always with,
my forever companion,
from here to eternity.

My God . . .
My Creator . . .
My Guide . . .
My Teacher . . .
My Protector . . .
My Mother . . .
My Father . . .
It is All in One . . .
It is You.
You.

My greatest love,
my deepest joy,
my profound peace . . .
Only, always . . .
it is You.

MIRACULOUS SILENCE

At times during meditation, your mind may wander, unable to embrace stillness. Instead of letting this frustration feed you, simply open your heart and let your breath guide you. There, in a moment, something miraculous can happen: you awaken to God.

STONES TO USE

AMETHYST: *to open the heart and mind*

FLUORITE: *to help diminish inner chatter and chaos*

MANTRA

Chant the name of the Divine, in any way that you wish

How can I be angry
while I sit at Your door?
I struggle as my mind wanders
to all my frustrations,
to all my trepidations,
to all my disappointments.

I fuel myself with this—
the agitation,
the anxiety of the next moment,
even before it arrives.
I feed my soul
the loud and constant chatter of voices.
I do this
even as I sit with You.

Then, slowly,
something magical happens . . .
In a moment,
the chatter stops.
Time holds still.
Anger dissipates.
Light emerges.
And there,
remain only You and I.

My body and mind relax
into the vast endlessness
of You.

You have patiently brought me
to this moment.
I thought this time
it would not happen again.
I was wrong.
I am here again,
with You.
You have never given up on me.

Even when I do not believe
in the calming silence
that I can have within me,
You show me how quiet
my inner world can be.
I am so content,
as I sit with You.

You are my God.

Beyond what
I can possibly understand or grasp,
You are the whole.

And once again,
I sit in awe,
in deep gratitude,
as You hold me
and my heart unfolds
into a miraculous silence . . .

unbelievable grace

Several years ago, there was a horrible earthquake in the Middle East. An entire region had virtually been wiped out, as houses and buildings were destroyed and thousands of lives were lost. I was asked to join a group of Middle Eastern artists for a benefit concert, in an effort to raise funds for the victims of this tragic event.

As we came together that evening in the concert hall, we sang our hearts out and channeled our grief into our instruments and music. We were all mourning the community's loss and our emotions were raw, but we did our best to keep our composure.

During the intermission, a famous singer we knew appeared backstage. He was dressed in black and looked devastated. At first, we thought he had shown up to participate in the event, but then we learned he had lost forty of his family members in the earthquake! His loss and grief were beyond anything we could have imagined. We all stood quietly, with tears in our eyes, unable to find any words of comfort to say to him.

The director of the event approached the singer, offered his condolences, then expressed how, under other circumstances, he would have loved for this singer to perform with us. The singer stunned the director when he replied, "Oh, but I can sing tonight! I want to honor the ones I have lost . . . and all those who have gone."

We were all startled by his offer to participate, not knowing how he could possibly perform under such extreme emotional distress. Would he even be able to sing? And if so, would he be able to withstand the avalanche of emotions and finish his song? We all stood at the side of the stage to show support and silently offer prayers of strength, as we all tried to will him to do well.

Miraculously, he was already connected to Source. He took the stage and delivered one of the most heartfelt and amazing vocal performances any of us had ever heard. We all wept openly, at the side of the stage, as his voice washed over an audience mesmerized by the strength and grace of this inspired performance. I'm sure there was not a tearless eye in sight.

Throughout his segment, his deep grief and devastation were apparent, but so were the love and light of God within him. When he got offstage, I gave him a big hug and asked, "How did you do that?"

He replied, "It was God's will. He carried me through it."

I just nodded my head, in knowing agreement. In his connection to God, he had magically delivered each of us to a place of Light. There was nothing more to say.

inspirational prayers

THE MIRACLE OF GOD IS YOU

"God, are You here? Why can I not see You? Why can I not feel You? I feel lost. Have You forgotten me? I sleep in unrest. My dreams are nightmares of my daily existence. I awake dreading the day. Time does not wait for me. I have waited for years; yet nothing has happened. I have no hope. I await a miracle."

Listen,
close your eyes,
open your arms,
breathe,
put your hand on your heart,
feel it pounding . . .

You are alive.

Open your eyes,
look around,
see the trees,
open the windows,
hear the rustling of the leaves,
feel the breeze . . .

This is the miracle . . .
Life.

Run your hands through cold water,
splash it on your face,
let your senses awaken . . .

This fresh sensation . . .
this
is Grace.

Step out,
look at the sky,
look at the stars gazing down.
Earth and Sky are your constant companions.
All around is life.
All hear you.
All feel you.
All see you.
You are never alone . . .

God is here,
each moment,
with you.

You are not seeing
the miracle He created . . .
the miracle that is *you.*

Your life is the miracle.
Your life is the biggest gift you have received.
All else pales in comparison.
What you are awaiting . . .
is *you.*

It is endless—
what you can have . . .
Do not limit yourself to external gifts.

The internal gifts
are much more fulfilling,
vast,
and infinite.

You have all the gifts of life.
You have the miracle of life . . .
being.

Now, open your eyes.
You will find God
everywhere . . .

His arms are embracing you . . .
You are His child always.

You . . .
are His miracle.

I BELIEVE IN ME

*There are days when we need to be reminded of how truly special we are,
of how beautifully the Divine has created us. As we see the truth within us,
our confidence will (re)emerge and we will embrace our higher self.*

STONES TO USE

JADE: *to promote wisdom, to connect us to the higher self*

RHODONITE: *to direct us to our truth and the Universe*

GIRASOL: *to support inner happiness*

ROSE QUARTZ: *to direct us to the love within*

CARNELIAN: *to honor the self*

MANTRA

Use passages of the prayer

Divine Father, Mother, God,
and so it is today . . .
the day I look in the mirror,
the day I am ready to see my truth,
the day I will bare my soul to myself
and hear its whisper.

I will love all my imperfections.
I will nurture all my strengths.
I will embrace all my challenges . . .
for I know I am here to grow.

I am here to find joy in small things . . .
those are what I will treasure the most.
And the big moments are glimpses of glory,
forever embedded in my memory.

But it is in feeling,
seeing,
and inhaling
all this beauty around me,
that I will once again know why I am here.

I am here to love.
I am here to spread joy.
I am here to embody light.
I am here to be a part of Creation.
I am here to elevate.

I can overcome all my challenges,
and when I feel unable to move forward,
I will allow my inner light to reawaken me,
as I connect more deeply to Spirit.

My growth is necessary,
for patterns that do not work need to shift.
My commitment to my spiritual being is essential,
for without it,
I will lose myself.

Today,
I look in the mirror and I see a beautiful me,
as created by You:
imperfect in every way that is perfect,
just as You intended . . .
Lovely, magnificent . . .
me.

Divinely woven,
from love,
with grace,
always and forever . . .
me.

Today is the day to start believing in *me*.

Spirit,
I behold this,
I behold life,
I behold You . . .
I behold me.

—◡—

FOR A MIRACLE

Miracles can happen each day. Wishes—big and small—can come true. However, we ourselves also need to take steps to help create and manifest our inner dreams, and trust that the Universe will guide us with Her infinite wisdom, as intended. Surrender your wish to God and trust in the will of the Divine.

STONES TO USE

FLUORITE/AMETHYST: *to open the inner channels*

TIGER'S EYE: *to support courage in taking positive action*

MANTRAS

"I trust Thy will"

"I surrender to the divine design"

SO HUM/HAM SA: *to connect to the seed of your being*

Anchor yourself and find your calm through your breath. Allow your mind to enter vastness. There, visualize your heart's desire and see the steps you can take to manifest your deepest wish. Embrace it.

Dear God,
Only You . . .
can make the impossible possible.
Only You . . .
can create the rains that nurture the earth.
Only You . . .
can create a radiant sun and an enticing moon.
Only You . . .
can create bright dancing stars in the dark carpet of night.
Only through Your hands . . .
may a sick child live and a blind man find sight.

Today, God,
I come to You to ask for a miracle . . .
I ask You this, dear God,
with a hopeful spirit:
[state what you wish for out loud]

I pray for this
from the depth of my being.
I pray for this
from the purest place within my heart.

This is my intention,
my wish.
Guide me,
show me
the ways I may manifest this,
and I will follow.

I pray for this miracle,
and yet,
I know that I must surrender it to You.
As I lay this prayer at Your door,
I know that I must trust
that my journey will unfold
as You intend.

Your will,
I shall accept.
I shall embrace.

Humbly I ask . . .
Humbly I bow.

Amen

THE REVIVAL OF THE SPIRIT

Sometimes we just need to allow ourselves to break down and cry. The soul needs to replenish itself. We need to let the tears wash away the haze, so that we may see clearly. Then once again, our belief in life and its magic is restored.

STONES TO USE

SNOW QUARTZ/GIRASOL (USE TOGETHER): *to bring forth inner joy and calm*

ROSE QUARTZ: *to foster self-love*

CARNELIAN: *to honor the self*

AMBER: *to soothe*

TURQUOISE: *to connect with the spiritual realm*

MOSS AGATE: *to heal, to bring forth inner harmony*

GARNET/RUBY: *to revitalize*

TOURMALINE: *to understand your placement in the Universe*

MANTRAS

"I trust, I believe, I shall rise again"

"I surrender to Thy will"

Mangala Charan Mantra: (see appendix A)

YA RAHMAN O YA RAHIM: *to call to the Benevolent*

Chant the name of the Divine, in any way that you wish

I knock on Your door,
yet I know,
it is always open.

I enter . . .
All is light . . .

I throw myself on the floor, sobbing.
So many questions my soul yearns to ask . . .
Why do we come?

Why do we go?
Why do we form such deep attachments
that are later taken from us?
And how can we bear so much heartache . . .
how?

Sobbing,
I look into the light.
It slowly embraces my folded body.
You lift me
and carry me.

I sob as You hold me.
I feel safe, secure.

"Cry," You say.
"I know you cannot understand,
for you belong to the earth.
When you reach the Kingdom of the Skies,
then you will understand . . .
There is no death,
there is no loss . . .
spirit remains always,
in one form or another.

"It is hard for your body to take in all this suffering,
but your spirit, through the ages,
has known deep sorrow and deep joy.
Much anguish you have endured;
yet you chose to come back,
for this life holds much beauty and love.
Even when you feel shattered,
you still choose to be . . .
All these gifts are known to the soul.
Now you are depleted . . .
Rest . . .

And as soon as you hear the birds
and smell the sweet scent of jasmine,
your weary soul will regain strength
and your spirit will rejoice in being,
once again.

"Trust me . . .
I know . . .
I see this each day and with each person.
You ask the same questions,
you cry the same pain,
and yet you rejoice and love this existence.

"My gift to you,
my child,
is this peace,
this deep embrace of love.
Let it settle within your being.
Hold it . . .
Close your eyes . . .
Know it . . .
Feel it . . .
And rest."

And so it was written, and so it was . . .

The scent of jasmine did awaken my senses,
and the glow of the sun did enliven me.
The birds and I sang joyously . . .
The pain drifted away . . .
Dreams and wishes rushed into my blood once again,
and then into my heart . . .

I skipped out . . .
I did not close the door,
for I knew another weary soul would soon enter.
I kissed the door . . .

I would be back . . .
Yes, several times . . .
But now, in this moment,
as I stood outside,
smelling the fresh green grass,
I knew . . .
I knew this gift of life was too precious to waste.

Joyously,
I ran into the meadows and plains . . .
I am here!
Life is grand!
Life is beautiful!
I am alive!
I am ready . . .
to embrace it all.

SOAR: LIBERATION OF THE SELF

Oh Spirit!
I am ready to fly!
I have found my wings.
I am ready to soar into the endless skies
and not look down,
for I am no longer afraid.

I never knew I could fly without hesitation.
I never knew there was a *me* who was unafraid.
I bow to You, oh Universe!

You have guided me to this . . .
to *me*.

I have found a new definition for my soul . . .
maybe it was my definition all along
and I did not know.

I want to shout it from the mountaintops.
I have come home!
I have come home within me.

I can dream again and reach greater heights.
I can sleep without knowing what the daylight holds.
I can see myself without layers of guilt and shame.

I am no longer afraid.
I am free,
ready to explore all there is.

I like myself . . .
I *love* myself . . .
for I have truly seen
that I am a reflection of the Light.
In this, I trust.
And I embrace it,
with all its glory!

I want to fly . . .
with no expectations,
with my heart open,
trusting in the magic of life.

I am ready,
Spirit . . .
I am ready!

I chant Your name,
as I sit with You in this Light,
and say in one breath . . .
I am free.

LOVE IS ALL WE NEED

We all come from Divine Love, and thus, we are love. Love is what sustains us all. Understanding this simple truth is key to opening our arms and embracing all that is.

STONES TO USE
ROSE QUARTZ / EMERALD: *to open the channels of love*

It is with Love that I come
and with Love that I shall leave.

It is love that I offer
and love that my heart craves.

It is love that awakens my soul
and love that quiets my mind in sleep.

It is love that ignites my spirit
and love lost that I grieve.

It is always love . . .
The divine gift from You.

All we need,
all we need to follow,
all we need to practice.

One word . . .
perfect, simple, universal,
all encompassing . . .
Love . . .
You.

I PRAY

I pray for the first sprinkle of spring rain
after a long winter's sleep,
refreshing my spirit with renewed hope.

I pray for the smell of morning dew
after a bitter-cold night,
awakening my senses with a gentle, sweet whisper.

I pray for the sun to pour in
after a thunderous evening,
as clouds drift away.

I pray for the sound of music that lifts my spirit
into a realm so beautiful and heavenly
that all else fades away.

I pray for a kiss from a beloved
that will make time stand still
and set my heart sailing
into a divine ocean of love.

I pray for the moment when my heart takes a leap
and life seems like a field
of endless adventure.

I pray . . .
I pray . . .
I pray for all the magic and wonder the heart can hold.

This is my prayer,
wrapped in love and joy . . .
I embrace this splendor
and behold Your grace.

FOR INSPIRATION

STONES TO USE

FLUORITE: *to awaken our inner dreams*

GIRASOL: *to bring forth happiness, to enhance creativity*

AMETHYST: *to open the channels within*

MANTRAS

"I embrace the wonder, I embrace the joy"

SO HUM/HAM SA: *to connect to the breath of being*

SATNAM: *to connect with your higher truth*

ONG SO HUNG: *to open the creative consciousness within*

Dear God,
I want to be inspired to new heights . . .
I want my spirit to soar
into a new awakening . . .

I want to feel alive
and full of wonder,
birthing new ideas and dreams . . .

I want to be captured
by adventures
beyond the realm of my imagination . . .

I pray to become one
with the pulse of the Universe,
rejoicing at the arrival of
dawn in my heart.

Beloved,
may I find this,
this inspiration . . .
within me,
around me,
in all I touch
and all I see . . .

May it brighten my life,
as I walk,
step by step,
into its embrace.

God,
I pray for this . . .
for the light within me
to glow brightly,
and for this to lead me
to the passion within my heart.

May it warm my being,
and in this,
may my soul be invigorated
with joy,
with hope,
in the days and nights ahead.

I behold and embrace
this wish,
this prayer.

And with this,
I shall remain.

Amen

~

FOR NEW DREAMS

At times, we may find that a dream we have held especially near and dear can no longer come true, and with this loss, we are forced to mourn a significant chapter in our lives. If we feel we have no other dreams left, we may feel especially defeated or depleted. In such moments, we must remain open, allowing the Universe to guide us to new colors, remembering that our hearts can bring forth new dreams.

STONES TO USE

FLUORITE: *to awaken to new dreams and wishes*

AMETHYST: *to open channels within*

JADE: *to heal, to protect*

LAPIS LAZULI: *to promote wisdom, truth, and self-discovery*

RUBY: *to bring resolution and empowerment after a period of disappointment*

MANTRAS

"I honor myself"

"I surrender to the divine design"

"I surrender to Thy will"

"I embrace the possibilities, full of joy and wonder"

"I behold my truth"

SO HUM/HAM SA: *to connect to the seed of your soul*

ONG SO HUNG: *to see the light within*

SATNAM: *to connect to your higher self and the Universe*

AAH: *to connect to your being, to promote confidence*

Chant the name of the Divine, in any way that you wish

MEDITATION/VISUALIZATION

Sit or lie down, and place one hand on your heart. Close your eyes and imagine a rainbow of colors surrounding you. Repeat the words "dreams . . . hope . . . life," inhaling and exhaling deeply each time.

Dear God,
I come to You today,
asking that You help me,
guide me,
as I mourn the end of an old dream . . .
one that could not be.

I feel depleted and defeated . . .
that which I held on to for so long
remains unfulfilled . . .
leaving an emptiness, a void,
within my soul.

As I let go of this dream,
I understand that I am freeing myself
to embrace a new vision,
a new path.

Oh Spirit,
help me heal . . .

Help me connect
with my higher self,
so I may find new hope,
new wishes,
and new colors
in my life.

With Your guidance,
I know I can release the old,
and embrace the endless possibilities
and adventures
of tomorrow . . .
and build new dreams,
once again.

Humbly,
I lay this prayer
at Your door,
and with Your grace,
I shall remain.

MIRACULOUS AGING

Aging can be beautiful if we honor the journey and live life in our truth. Some cultures place an exaggerated emphasis on youth, while in others getting older earns one respect and credibility in the community. With age, we become wiser and more enlightened, able to live each day more liberated and better aligned with our higher truth. This is the miracle of aging.

STONES TO USE

ROSE QUARTZ / CARNELIAN: *to honor the self*

MANTRAS

"Each day I am more whole"

"I am free"

"Soul is ageless"

"Time brings wisdom"

"I surrender to the wisdom of the Universe"

"I embrace Thee"

SO HUM / HAM SA: *to connect to the breath
    of being*

SATNAM: *to connect to your higher self*

Oh Spirit,

You have traveled with me for many years . . .

You have seen me learn and grow.

You have seen me laugh.

You have seen me hurt.

Many a day,

You have seen me struggle within myself.

Many a night,

You have lay by my side

as I questioned my life,

my dreams.

Fear was my companion for many moons . . .

I held on to her,

scared to reveal my heart's inner truth

to myself.
I let her stop me.

I excused many who bruised my heart.
I gave them second and third chances,
not feeling worthy.
I did not honor myself.

I sat in turmoil,
at the core of my being,
not seeing or allowing myself to emerge,
denying myself, of my truth,
of *me* . . .

Searching constantly . . .
for who I was,
what I wanted,
and where I fit in,
I wandered through
the many dark hallways of my mind . . .

With each passing season,
I caught a better glimpse of who I truly am,
relinquishing fear,
piece by piece,
embracing new knowledge
and wisdom gained
through the gift of time.

Today,
as I look in the mirror,

I see a face that reflects the passage of time.
I have earned each wrinkle,
each white hair,
each pause in my step,
through the tears and laughter
of seasons past.

The lines etched on my face . . .
each tells a story
from the treasure chest
of my memories,
each speaks of an adventure

my heart has known,
each reveals a different color
in the tapestry of my life.

The once-young child,
now mature and wiser,
has walked a long road,
many times falling,
but always rising.

I have learned
that I will not always receive answers
to my questions.

I have lived
long enough to know
that the heart always heals.

I have lived
long enough to know
that time never holds still.

I have gained knowledge through You.
I have found confidence through You.
I have strengthened my faith through You.
I have seen my true self through You.

I have gained wisdom to know
that this life
is our most precious gift
from the Divine.

I know not when it happened . . .
Was it in an instant,
in a moment of time,
while taking a brisk autumn walk,
or in the sacred space of meditation and prayer?
I know not.
I just know it happened . . .
Through Your love,
I came home to myself.

Today,
fear is behind me.
With the insecurities of youth long gone,
my wings are ready for flight.
I finally feel free.
I now breathe with an ease
I never knew before.
I feel happy
just to be with *me*.

No explanations do I offer,
no excuses,
no desire to please . . .
I am comfortable just to be
myself.

Spirit,
You and I have journeyed so far,
and I look forward to what lies ahead . . .
I want to live,
embracing each moment,

of my remaining days and years,
building new dreams,
making new memories . . .

I want to soar!

Oh Spirit,
today liberation is finally upon me,
as I have freed myself
from my limitations.

In each turn,
in each season,
celebrating life . . .
celebrating magic . . .
celebrating the gift of aging.

I bow to You in gratitude.

Shokran

SISTERS

*Women are like the soil that nourishes a beautiful garden. We are the
pillars; we are the whisper of higher intuition. In turmoil, and in the
twists and turns of life, let us remember not only our own strength but
also that of the thread that weaves us all together. From the Divine, we*

have come to be the nurturers, and in such light, we remain always—
woven together with loving strength.

Oh Spirit,
You gave us life.
We bow to You.
Hear our whisper,
our story . . .

In the womb,
we learned of patience
from our mother.

Every time she lovingly
caressed her belly,
we knew and understood love.

Each time she lay awake at night,
thinking and worrying
about those she loved,
we understood what
caring was.

Separate,
yet interwoven
we were,
understanding
that the love that resides
between us
was deeper than time,

stronger than mountains,
richer than gold.

And so it began . . .
Even before we knew who we were,
we knew
that we had come here to love,
to care,
to be the home of children,
the hope of elders,
and the voice of the meek.

We came onto this earth and grew.
We felt with all our hearts . . .
we loved with fervor,
we cried from the depth of our beings,
and we cared with all we were.

In each turn,
we danced with the winds,
or fell to our knees in heartache,
and there,
we saw faces,
mirrors of our own . . .

We saw our sisters,
carrying Your light
within their eyes.

One image
upon each face,

upon the mirror—
strong,
all encompassing,
courageous and kind,
undeniable . . .
You.

Connected by this sacred thread,
interwoven through time,
through life,
through love . . .
all of us from You.
Created as women,
blessed to be
in the divine chain of sisterhood.

We pray,
oh Spirit . . .
We pray
for all our sisters
across the seas and lands . . .

May they be honored
as the light they are.
May they stand, not alone
but together,
under Your shield of grace.

May their souls carry wisdom,
their hearts teach love,
and their eyes see the truth

that they each hold,
the only truth that *is* . . .
You.

May they remain in safety
and be protected from harm.
May they see their beauty,
know their strength,
and know the goodness and love
that reside in their souls.

Oh Spirit,
as sisters You created us,
and as such
we shall remain,
through winds and rains,
through storms and sunshine,
through moons and years,
under Your guiding light,
always as a chain . . .
Sisters,
woven
by one thread . . .
You.

Shokran

YOU WHO ARE MOTHER

Mothers are the pillars of life, and have a sacred place in God's kingdom, for it is through their loving hearts that we better see the love that resides within us.

To you, who cares . . .
To you, who loves . . .
To you, who nurtures . . .

To you, who makes hope from despair . . .
To you, who makes laughter from tears . . .
To you, who makes home from mud . . .

To you, who plants seeds of love . . .
To you, who is present even when far . . .
To you, who lives forever in the heart . . .

I behold you, for you are divinely woven.
I behold you, for you are pure love.
I behold you, for you are mother.

From you, there is life.
From you, there is hope.
From you, there is grace.

Throughout the lands,
and across the seas,
it is known:
you sit in the heart of God.

You, mother . . .
always treasured,
always cherished,
of the Divine,
of Love . . .

Forever,
embraced by Light . . .
I behold your love,
always.

Namaste*

FOR PARENTS OF A CHILD
WITH SPECIAL NEEDS

Individuals who are "different" are sometimes misunderstood by society. It takes wisdom and insight for us to see that these individuals are not only here to teach us but also to help us elevate. Their uniqueness is a blessing upon us, the essence of their being makes our lives richer, and their purity humbles us.

Note: please replace "he," "him," and "son" with "she," "her," and "daughter" if applicable.

"My dear child,
I wish you to hear Me.

---

* Hindi phrase interpreted here as "I bow to you." Derived from the Sanskrit *nama*, meaning "to bow," and *te*, meaning "to you."

I have chosen a special being
to be your son.

"I have made him
from a different cloth,
with a different touch.
I have designed him beautifully,
in unique colors.

"The day I created him,
I knew the world needed
those like him,
who are here on earth
for a very special reason:
to be the light,
to be the messengers of My love.

"He is not less than
but *more* than anyone can imagine.
He is not unloved
but loved beyond measure.

"Not everyone can see
his remarkable heart.
Not everyone can see
his brilliant mind,
and his unique ways
of looking at things.

Do not question
why he is different,
but remember,
that his *difference* is what will teach
and help others
to see beyond themselves.
It is his *gift* . . .
to be different from most,
to live differently than most.

Some,
with wisdom
and a more generous heart,
will truly see him,
and embrace him;
others will slowly learn from him
and become more enlightened for it.
But all who cross his path
will be touched by him,
and will be richer for it.

Find peace in knowing
that I have a special love
for him in my heart,
that my heavenly angels
will always look after him
and embrace him.

Remember . . .
your child is beautiful

and blessed . . .
In my garden of Creation,
he is my radiant flower.

Remind him
to be true to himself,
to know that he is my special child
forever,
and always.

MAGICAL SURRENDER

What lies around the next corner? It could be magic! At any moment your life may ignite with love, with magical possibilities. Close your eyes and believe in the divine tapestry that has been created so beautifully— full of colors and patterns beyond your vision. Surrender to its design.

MANTRA
*"I believe . . .
in You,
in the magic of life,
in the magic of me,
in the hope of it all . . .
I believe"*

I know not what tomorrow will bring;
yet I know it will be different
than whatever I imagine.

I know not who I will meet
or with whom I will journey.

I know not what the day will hold
or what the night will whisper.

Not knowing what lies ahead
excites me and gives me hope . . .

For I know You are always with me.

I believe . . .
I have hope . . .
hope that there will be
rainbows, colors, and dreams . . .
beyond what I could ever imagine.

And with this hope,
I surrender . . .
to the magic of life
and to Your divine design.

a knowing soul,
graced by faith

As I looked around the room at one of my intuitive and channeling workshops, I saw many unfamiliar faces, people sitting and hoping for a message. Among the many faces, I did recognize one—a beautiful actress I had met once before. I remembered that she and her husband were very accomplished in their craft and had a comfortable and affluent life with two lovely children. I also could not help but notice another woman, one whose face was unfamiliar to me but whose presence could not be ignored. She was captivating and full of life, with a beauty that seemed to emanate from deep within.

Toward the end of the session, many attendees were asking me questions, and this entrancing woman was happily contributing her feedback with a depth of wisdom and an unstoppable smile. As she was speaking with a radiant energy that permeated the room, the actress turned to her and asked, "What makes you so happy? What do you have in your life that brings you such joy? What is your secret?"

The woman responded by telling us about her life: she was living with very minimal finances, had lost her mother a year before, had no major career and no partner. And yet she was filled with joy. When she saw the look of confusion on the faces of the others in the room, she added, "The reason I am happy is because, despite it all, I have *me*, and I have all *this*," she said, extending her arms open. "I have the Universe and all Her gifts."

Surprised and clearly emotional, the actress said, "I have all the comforts in life. I have lovely children. I have a wonderful husband. And yet I am always depressed. I wish I had *this* . . . this belief that you do . . . this joy that you have."

At the close of the session, this mesmerizing woman flowed out of the class as each strand of her long, jet-black hair danced with timeless energy. We were left affected, inspired, and in awe—our senses awakened. I knew the other participants would have traded all the riches in the world—all the comforts they had—for an ounce of *that*.

For years, and throughout the world, I have shared this story—about the woman who *appeared* to have nothing but yet had everything . . . for she had faith in herself and life.

prayers
for healing

FOR CLARITY

Sometimes our minds and hearts cannot see clearly. At such times, we can gently caress our spirits and remind ourselves that the haze will clear. We will come to a place of clarity—if not today, then in time.

STONES TO USE

FLUORITE: *to quiet the inner chatter*

AMETHYST: *to open the channels of inner vision, to promote awareness*

SODALITE: *to sharpen the mind*

LAPIS LAZULI: *to see with wisdom*

MOOKAITE: *to find the right pathways*

CARNELIAN: *to honor the self, to empower*

MANTRAS

"I am truth"

"I see me"

SO HUM / HAM SA: *to connect to the self and the Universe*

AAH: *to invoke confidence*

ONG SO HUNG: *to open yourself to the light within*

NAM MYOHO RENGE KYO: *to empower, to invoke confidence as we connect to the Universe*

Chant the name of the Divine, in any way that you wish

MEDITATION/VISUALIZATION

(OPTIONAL: "FLAME MEDITATION" WITH THE USE OF A CANDLE)

(RECOMMENDED ADDITION: "WALKING MEDITATION")

Use your breath to calm your mind and its chatter. Sit in the quiet of being. Embrace this stillness, and slowly you will hear the whisper of your soul. Embrace this joy and peace.

Oh Beloved,
I come to You today seeking guidance,
so that I may see the road in front of me clearly.

My vision is blurred,
and I am scared to make a wrong turn,
a wrong decision.

Please shed Your light upon my path,
so I can walk through it with more clarity,
so I can choose with greater wisdom.

Please help me clear
the clutter in my head
and in my heart.
Help me lift this burden from my shoulders.

Oh God,
I pray to hear the whisper of truth,
to allow it,
to embrace it.

Through Your light,
I know I will see more clearly,
and there,
with You,
I will find my answers.

In Your light,
I sit.

Amen

RELEASING THOUGHTS AND
EMOTIONS THAT DO NOT SERVE US

Thoughts and emotions such as rage, jealousy, revenge, resentment, shame, and unfounded guilt are often rooted in a lack of self-worth and self-love, and are disruptive to the spirit, eating away at the soul. In addition to seeking the help of a counselor, practicing daily walking meditation and using mantras can be key to understanding and releasing these negative emotions and thoughts.

STONES TO USE

OBSIDIAN: *to help break down barriers within, to cleanse and heal*

RHODONITE: *to support the release of negative thoughts*

MOSS AGATE: *to release negative feelings and limitations*

SNOW QUARTZ: *to restore calm*

GARNET: *to stimulate positive energy*

ROSE QUARTZ: *to forgive and love oneself*

TURQUOISE: *to connect to the higher self*

MANTRAS

"I am a child of God. I am special. I am loved"

"I am the breath of Love"

OM AH HUM: *to awaken to all there is in the Universe*

HO'OPONOPONO: *to reconcile, to forgive*

SATNAM: *to release uncomfortable feelings, to connect to the light within*

OM: *to find balance and center*

HUMATA, HUKHTA, HUVARSHTA, SVAH: *for purification of thoughts, actions, and words*

Chant the name of the Divine, in any way that you wish

Calm your mind through your breath and allow it to drift into a vast field of nothingness. Focus on your heart center, see the light that is there—a warm healing light. Fill your being with this light. As you inhale, receive its joy. As you exhale, allow your body to relax further. Inhale love, peace, kindness, and joy until you find your inner calm.

Dear God,
I come to You,
for I am tormented.
I am unsettled,
with feelings and thoughts
that overwhelm me.
I know not how
to escape them.

I feel my soul is ignited by a fire
that can harm me
and, at times,
hurt others.
Yet, I know *this* is not
who I truly am.
I am not a burning flame
but a loving sea . . .
created by You.

Oh Spirit,
I turn to You,
to come to a deeper knowing of myself,
so I may wash away that which creates

such anguish and discontent
within me.

Please guide me
so I may quiet my mind
and calm my spirit . . .
so I may unleash my restless soul
and release this pain
into an ocean of healing tears . . .

God,
help me forgive, mourn, and grieve.
Help me release the disappointments,
the heartaches,
the insecurities
that have stirred such emotions
in my soul,
eating away at my core.

I wish to let them go
and to replace them
with a loving peace . . .
breathing in Your love.

God,
I sit at Your door,
asking that You help bring me
to this calm.
Please deliver me
to the light that resides within me,
so my mind can rest,

so my heart can beat
with the peaceful rhythm of Your love.

Help me remember
that I am worthy,
that I can be happy and at peace,
that I can love myself . . .
for I am of Love,
for I am
of *You*.

I sit in Your light,
oh God,
and ask that You please
guide me to this.

Amen

COPING WITH REGRET

STONES TO USE

FLUORITE: *to quiet the inner chatter of the mind*

ROSE QUARTZ: *to promote self-love, forgiveness, and acceptance*

CARNELIAN: *to empower, to honor*

RHODONITE: *to resolve matters of the heart*

RUBY: *to empower, to honor, to create healing*

MANTRAS

"I trust Thy will"

HO'OPONOPONO: *to forgive*

YA RAHMAN O YA RAHIM: *to call to the Benevolent*

NAM MYOHO RENGE KYO: *to revive the self, to empower*

SATNAM: *to sit in your higher truth*

Chant the name of the Divine, in any way that you wish

Dear God,

I sit in turmoil,

in anguish,

for my heart and mind

are filled with regret

about things I cannot change,

about things I cannot undo.

I am tormented

by the questions,

the doubts,

that race through my mind

and create unrest within me.

I know I cannot

turn back the hands of time.

I know I cannot

change my actions or choices.

And yet,

these thoughts

whirl in my heart and mind.

Oh Spirit,
I do not wish to judge myself.
I do not wish to feel anger or guilt
about what has been.
I wish to be free . . .
free from my expectations,
harsh judgments,
and blame . . .
Free from regret.

I turn to You,
oh God . . .
Please show me
the way to healing.
Guide me to this,
and help me release
this pain.

Help me understand
that I need not suffer like this,
that I can forgive myself
for that which I wish
were different.

Help me
wash away my guilt,
relinquish my self-doubt,
and accept that which has been,
so I may reach a place of peace
within me.

Oh Spirit,
help me remember
that there is wisdom
to the divine design,
and that I must trust
that I have always
been guided.

I will honor my path, Beloved . . .
I will trust the hands of the Universe,
and the angels,
who have led my way
each day.

As I sit with You,
I know I will find new hope.
I will find my peace,
and through this
I will journey to a place
of acceptance, of clarity,
and a newfound calm.

I know I will heal.
I trust this.
Your will I embrace.

FOR FORGIVENESS

Forgiveness is an act—a journey of steps. It takes time to understand, heal, release, and finally forgive. Allow yourself this space and know that as you forgive those who hurt you, you will find your own liberation and self-love.

STONES TO USE

AMETHYST: *to promote awareness*

MOONSTONE: *to open our hearts to forgiveness*

MOSS AGATE: *to remove anger and guilt*

ROSE QUARTZ: *to heal emotional scars*

JASPER: *to protect from negative thoughts*

RHODONITE: *to open and resolve matters of the heart*

CARNELIAN: *to empower yourself*

MANTRAS

HO'OPONOPONO: *to forgive, to reconcile feelings*

OM MANI PADME HUM: *to forgive, to allow compassion*

SO HUM/HAM SA: *to connect to the breath of life and the Universe*

Chant the name of the Divine, in any way that you wish

Note: please replace "he" and "him" with "she" and "her" if applicable.

Oh Spirit,
I know not how to let go
of these feelings
of hurt and resentment,
which fuel me at all hours . . .
I know not how to forgive.

I no longer wish
to harbor this pain . . .
it does not serve me.

I no longer want
to keep this hurt,
this anger
that has coiled around me,
sitting at my core,
stopping me from feeling joy,
from feeling peace,
from moving forward.

I wish to embrace Love,
at each turn.
I wish to understand
the lessons life teaches us.
I wish to restore my peace.
I wish to elevate.

God,
I know it is only
through Your grace
that I can see clearly
and find my steps,
one at a time . . .
into a place of forgiveness.

Please guide me
to Your light
within me,

so I can forgive [name of the person],
so I can bless him,
as he continues his journey.

I embrace You,
oh Spirit,
and am ready
to liberate myself
from these chains.
Guide me,
to break free.

Shokran

TO RELEASE FEAR

Fear is a frequent companion for many of us, one that often stops us from living the life we wish. Once we recognize the root of our fear, we can understand it better and begin the healing process. Slowly thereafter, our fear will subside and our soul will celebrate its liberation.

STONES TO USE

ROSE QUARTZ/AMETHYST: *to open us to a loving channel within ourselves*

AQUAMARINE/OBSIDIAN/RHODONITE/TOURMALINE: *to help release blockages, to release self-limitations*

CARNELIAN/JASPER: *to feel grounded and secure*

LAPIS LAZULI: *to aid in self discovery*

MALACHITE/TOPAZ: *to strengthen*

TIGER'S EYE: *to enhance courage*

RUBY: *to empower, to bring forth courage*

ONYX: *to contain emotions*

HEMATITE/ARAGONITE: *to relieve intense anxiety*

MANTRAS

"I am not of fear, I am of Love"

AAH: *to connect to the self, to support confidence*

Judaic Mantra for Fear (see appendix A)

SATNAM: *to release anxiety and connect to your higher truth*

NAM MYOHO RHENGE KYO: *to energize, to empower*

Chant the name of the Divine, in any way that you wish

MEDITATION/VISUALIZATION

(OPTIONAL: "FLAME MEDITATION" WITH THE USE OF A CANDLE)

(RECOMMENDED ADDITION: "WALKING MEDITATION")

Inhale and exhale slowly. Center yourself in a peaceful calm. Envision a vast green field, full of colorful flowers. See yourself dancing in the field, joyous, happy, and liberated. See a halo of light around you. Embrace it and feel its loving calm. Slowly envision that which you fear. Take deep inhalations, and as you exhale, see yourself releasing your fear through your breath. Do this three or four times, until you feel the fear is dissolving. Once again, find your calm and sit in peace. Each time you repeat this, you will feel a greater sense of liberation from fear.

Dear God,

I have sat with fear

for many years of my life.

I have been scared . . .

of living life fully,

of making decisions,
of creating movement.
Fear has left me paralyzed and frozen,
unable to move ahead.

I wish to live a fulfilling life,
liberating myself
from these chains of anxiety.

I wish to release my fear,
oh Spirit,

and give it to the winds to carry
into the oceans of Your love.

I wish to embrace
all the bountiful gifts
and blessings
You have bestowed upon me.

I wish to see
the endless beauty,
the endless possibilities,
that lie before me.

Help me,
dear God . . .
help me find the courage,
the confidence,
the faith and belief,
to let go
of the negative patterns of thought
that hinder my growth,
my life.

Help me remember
that I am worthy,
that I am capable . . .
of being happy,
of being fulfilled,
of being at peace.

Oh Spirit,
I pray to believe in myself,
and to understand that the light
that resides within me
is of Love.
I want to see myself,
as You see me.

I pray to sit with *You*, not fear.
I pray to embrace *You*, not fear.
I pray to live with *You*, not fear.

God,
I am ready.
I am ready to begin a new chapter,
free and liberated . . .
from fear.

And in Your light,
I shall remain.

Shokran

~~~

FOR ONE WITH PHOBIAS

A phobia is an irrational fear, a manifestation of anxiety. For those who have phobias, these fears seem very real, and can result in panic attacks and/or feelings of being frozen. Psychotherapy and hypnosis are effective tools that can help in healing. Daily meditation and visualization can also support and build confidence and security—in time, lessening anxiety and fears.

STONES TO USE

AQUAMARINE: *to ease anxiety and phobia*

HEMATITE: *to reduce hysteria*

ARAGONITE: *to open to a new vision, to reduce high stress*

CARNELIAN: *to empower*

MOSS AGATE: *to support the removal of restrictive feelings*

ROSE QUARTZ: *to honor the self*

MALACHITE: *to strengthen our reserve*

ONYX: *to contain our emotions*

JASPER: *to ground, to protect from negative energies*

OBSIDIAN: *to guide you to the root of blockages, to break the blockages*

MANTRAS

"I am not of fear, I am of Love"

OM TARE TUTTARE TURE SOHA: *to remove blockages*

SO HUM / HAM SA: *to connect to the seed of the soul*

SATNAM: *to connect to the higher self*

Judaic Mantra for Fear (see appendix A)

Chant the name of the Divine, in any way that you wish

MEDITATION/VISUALIZATION

(OPTIONAL: "FLAME MEDITATION" WITH THE USE OF A CANDLE)

(RECOMMENDED ADDITION: "WALKING MEDITATION")

Find your calm through your breath. Imagine yourself in a green field or the ocean. Surround yourself with a golden white light. Be gentle, kind, and loving to yourself. Visualize yourself coming face-to-face with your fear. Breathe. Repeat this daily until you feel you have lessened your fear. Feel the elation, confidence, and empowerment.

Oh dear God,
I am so afraid.
In this moment,
my mind is
questioning my abilities,
testing my reserves,
draining me
of my self-belief.

I know not
when fear became me
and I became fear.
But now,
I can smell it on my breath,
I can taste it on my lips,
I can hear it
in the whisper
of the walls within me . . .

God,
please lead me to healing . . .
help me quiet my mind,
calm my soul,
and turn the whisper of fear
into a song of love,
and the mirage of darkness
into a stream of light.

Lead me to my core,
to my center,

to the child within me . . .
who is not afraid,
who loves life,
who is free.

Please hold my hand,
oh Spirit.
With Your light
and Your guidance,
I will find strength
and courage.
I will find my way.

I will not judge myself,
for I know,
You do not judge me.
I know I am of Light,
I am of You.

I will face this.
I will release this—
this which holds me
without an escape . . .
for I am not *this*.

I am not this fear.
I am not this anxiety.
I am love.
I am capable.
I am able to liberate myself

from these chains of fear.
I am of Love . . .
of Light . . .
I am of You.

I will chant
and I will believe:
I can . . .
and I will . . .
be free.

I will be free.

FOR A SOUL IN CRISIS

At any stage of life, we may experience a crisis of the soul. This usually happens when we are not living our higher truth or have had a series of disappointments, leading to deep frustration. The soul starts calling, and then screaming, demanding that we pay attention. The guidance of a counselor or a spiritual teacher, as well as the practice of daily meditation and prayer, during such periods can help us understand ourselves, find the path of our truth, and work through the aspects of our lives that need to be healed and changed.

STONES TO USE

MOSS AGATE: *to restore the spirit*

ARAGONITE: *to open yourself to new visions*

FLUORITE: *to recognize dreams*

LAPIS LAZULI: *to be awakened to the higher truth*

SODALITE: *to help connect to wisdom and new perceptions*

CARNELIAN: *to empower, to support our dreams and action*

GIRASOL: *to bring forth joy*

SNOW QUARTZ: *to calm*

OBSIDIAN/RHODONITE: *to remove obstacles*

ONYX/JASPER/TOURMALINE: *to ground*

RUBY/GARNET: *to revitalize, to bring forth liberation*

MANTRAS

"I honor myself"

"I am worthy"

"I am the breath of God"

SATANAMA: *to release blockage, to connect to our soul's purpose and journey*

SATNÁM: *to honor the self*

NAM MYOHO RENGE KYO: *to connect to the Universe, to bring empowerment*

SO HUM/HAM SA: *to connect to the breath of being*

YA HAYY O YA HAQQ: *the call for truth*

Chant the name of the Divine, in any way that you wish

MEDITATION/VISUALIZATION

(OPTIONAL: "FLAME MEDITATION" WITH THE USE OF A CANDLE)

(RECOMMENDED ADDITION: "WALKING MEDITATION")

Breathe in slowly. Exhale all your stress and anxiety. Put your hand on your heart and feel it beating. See yourself immersed in a healing white light. Feel its love and warmth within and all around you. Embrace this with your being. Visualize this light guiding your way back to your true self. Believe.

Oh Dívine,
I feel torn on the inside . . .
Angst is upon my soul.
It takes my breath away
and awakens me from sleep.

My frustration is deeper than the waters
that run through Your earth,
and my confusion
is embedded in the grains of my being.

I am in constant turmoil,
not knowing how to uncoil this snake
that is wrapped around my heart.

I did not listen to the whispers
of my unrest . . .
I did not nurture the tears
that had nested in my eyes . . .
I did not.

Today,
dear God,
I pray for guidance—
guidance to know how
to walk through the haze,
to sit with this unrest,
to reclaim the seed from which
I have sprung.

I am praying
that I can find *me*

and nurture the tears
that will release my anguish.

I wish to peel off
the layers
that do not serve me.

I hope that,
through the tides,
I will see the brink of a new shore,
a new day.

I know I can.
I know with Your love,
with Your grace,
with Your guidance,
I can.
I will.

I will stand strong
with my truth.
I will rest peacefully
within my soul,
in joy,
finding my path,
my purpose,
at this crossroads.

Oh soul,
I caress you,
I am listening . . .

I am here,
once again,
loving you.

And with this,
I shall sit,
awaiting the light
to pour in.

Shokran

FOR THOSE WHO HAVE LOST
BELIEF IN THEMSELVES

There is always someone who never gives up on you, someone who believes in you. This person may be alive or in the spirit world. In either case, remember: when you cannot dream, when you cannot believe someone, somewhere, is rooting for you.

STONES TO USE

AMBER/GIRASOL: *to lift your spirit and bring inner tranquility*

JADE: *to anchor*

MOSS AGATEM/OBSIDIAN: *to help release fear and restrictive feelings*

ROSE QUARTZ/CARNELIAN: *to promote self-love, to honor the self*

RHODONITE: *to open the channels to healing within*

RUBY/GARNET: *to revitalize, to replenish*

MALACHITE/ONYX/TOURMALINE: *to ground, to strengthen*

MANTRAS

"I am the breath of Love, I am of Light"
"I am loved by God"
"Someone always believes in me"
SO HUM/HAM SA: *to connect to the breath of life*
HO'OPONOPONO: *to reconcile with self*
YA RAHMAN O YA RAHIM: *to call to the Benevolent*
Chant the name of the Divine, in any way that you wish

MEDITATION/VISUALIZATION
(OPTIONAL: "FLAME MEDITATION" WITH THE USE OF A CANDLE)
(RECOMMENDED ADDITION: "WALKING MEDITATION")

Imagine you are sitting in a field of green with wildflowers around you. Feel the warmth of the sun. Envision its radiant light embracing you. Become one with this. Breathe in self-love, and see yourself as part of the beautiful divine design. Exhale this love and release all doubt and fear. Believe.

When did you decide to give up on yourself?
When was enough pain enough?

When did you replace love with fear
and dreams with nightmares?

When did you become scared to sit with yourself
and look within?

I know you feel lost,
and at this moment
cannot see the light within you . . .
If I could take away your pain,

I would.
If I could heal your scars,
I would.
If I could make a rainbow of colors,
and gift each color to you,
I would.

I believe . . .

I know
that God is with you,
embracing you,
and guiding your way at all times,
even when you cannot see
or feel Him.

I believe . . .

You are never alone . . .
God always sits with you,
rests with you,
and lifts you
when you cannot stand.

I believe in you.

I know that you shall rise from this,
that each tear shall birth many smiles,
that you will feel the rays of hope
stream into your heart.

I believe in you . . .

I can see your beautiful inner light,
and see how special you are . . .
I believe that you are magical
and full of talents and gifts within.

I believe in the beauty,
wonder,
and colors
that life can bring you . . .

And I will dream for you,
for I know you have stopped dreaming.
I will wish for you,
for I know you are depleted.
I will pray for you,
for I know you feel lost.

I will believe *in* you.
I will believe *for* you.
I believe . . .
and I know that one day soon,
you, too, will once again
believe
in *you*.

I trust this,
I know this,
I breathe this,
and with this,

I shall remain in prayer,
for you.

Namaste

COPING WITH A LOVED ONE
WHO REFUSES HELP

There are many individuals who either ignore or feel incapable of con-fronting their pain, illnesses, or challenges. With time, their lack of commitment, insight, or desire to heal may take a physical and/or emotional toll on their families and others around them. It is very dif-ficult to help those who do not want to be helped, and the hardest part of loving them is in knowing when to let go. We cannot "fix" a loved one; the plea for help must come from within.

Seeking help from support groups and therapists can be a source of relief and healing to you and your loved one. Prayer, meditation, and creating sacred space can further help build stronger reserves, faith, and patience—making your everyday life more bearable and shielding you from the toxicity of negative feelings and situations.

STONES TO USE

ARAGONITE: *to open to new visions*

CARNELIAN: *to empower, to calm*

RUBY/GARNET: *to empower, to honor, to renew*

MALACHITE/ONYX: *to relieve exhaustion, to rejuvenate*

ZOISITE: *to ease exhaustion, to relieve lethargy*

CALCITE: *to heal, to stimulate the positive within*

TOURMALINE/JASPER: *to ground*
TOPAZ: *to strengthen*

MANTRAS
"I surrender to Thy will"
"I trust the journey we each have, I trust"
Chant the name of the Divine, in any way that you wish

> *Note: please replace "he" and "him" with*
> *"she" and "her" if applicable.*

Dear Beloved,
Light of Lights,
You who govern the days and nights,
You who reside within our hearts,
I come to You today,
tired and confused,
not knowing how
to relieve my loved one
from this suffering,
and not knowing how to cope
with this constant anguish and depletion . . .

I love him,
oh God,
but this illness that has plagued him
has also wrapped around my body,
like a snake.
I can feel the sting,
the venom in my blood,

drowning my senses,
stealing my strength,
and poisoning my mind.

Oh God,
please receive my pain,
my heart,
my prayers . . .
How do I help heal him,
he who does not wish to be healed?

I pray,
with all I am,
for him,
for his awakening . . .
that he may see that he is unwell,
and know that
he can heal from this.

I pray that his bondage will be broken,
and that I, too,
will feel hopeful once again,
and liberated from these chains.

Dear God,
guide us to this . . .
Awaken him from this slumber,
and strengthen me to love myself
as I love him.

Thank you,
oh Beloved,
for the blessing of prayer.
This sacred space
is my anchor.

With this,
I will continue each day,
trusting the journey we each have . . .

To Thy will,
I surrender.

Shokran

FOR ONE WHO IS CONTEMPLATING SUICIDE

*A mind that sits in darkness cannot see clearly. If you are contemplating suicide, please know that if you receive the proper treatment, your perception **will** shift. Reach out for help—a suicide hotline, support groups, friends and family members, health practitioners. And turn to prayer several times a day, remembering that God is always with you. Give Him your pain and sit in prayer. Allow faith to anchor you. No matter how hard it appears at this moment, you can overcome these thoughts and feelings, and find the path to healing and a fulfilling life. You will find the light within. Things can and will feel better. You can find joy of being, inspiration, motivation, and hope, as your perception shifts. Believe . . . God never leaves you.*

STONES TO USE

HEMATITE: *to help reduce escalated anxieties, to bring balance*

ARAGONITE: *to open you to a new vision, to support you in times of high stress*

CARNELIAN: *to empower, to help you honor yourself, to protect*

JASPER: *to protect from negative thought patterns*

JADE: *to heal, to promote secure feelings*

MOSS AGATE/RHODONITE: *to help heal, to help release negative feelings*

ROSE QUARTZ: *to promote self-love*

TURQUOISE: *to connect to your higher self, to protect*

GIRASOL/SNOW QUARTZ: *to bring forth the light of joy within you, to foster a state of calm*

RUBY/GARNET: *to revitalize the self, to create vitality*

MANTRAS

"I am the child of God, God is always with me"

"My life is of importance, my life has higher purpose"

"I shall overcome this, I will find my light, I will find my joy, I believe"

"God never leaves me"

YA SHAFEE O YA KHAFEE: *to call onto God, the Healer*

OM TARE TUTTARE TURE SOHA: *to remove mental, emotional, and physical obstacles*

SO HUM/HAM SA: *to connect to the breath of life and Creation*

SATNAM: *to release negative energies, to connect to the inner light*

OM AH HUM: *to embrace the light of the Universe*

OM HANSAM HANSAHA: *to promote good health*

Gayatri Mantra (see appendix A)

NAM MYOHO RENGE KYO: *to revitalize, to rejuvenate the self*

Chant the name of the Divine, in any way that you wish

Take deep inhalations and exhalations. Allow your mind to find quiet. Put your hand on your heart and feel it beating—this is your divine gift. Close your eyes and feel a light within you . . . a radiant golden light expanding throughout your entire being. Embrace this. This is God. Remember that you are here for a divine reason. Believe in this. Give your pain and anguish to God. Feel His love cradle you.

Spirit,
all seems dark.
I long to escape this . . .
this existence.

How can I rise again?
How can I laugh again?
How can I dream again?
How can I ever find my way?

The darkest of thoughts
occupy my mind,
and I feel a deep hopelessness,
a desire to give up.
I feel I do not have any more
strength within me,
to fight this battle of life.

My mind languishes in depression.
My heart feels only darkness.
All feels senseless.
My soul feels only decay.

I wish not to be anymore—
I do not want this breath,
I do not want this life,
I want to be free from my misery . . .
I feel I cannot bear this any longer.

God,
I am turning to You . . .
You who created me,
who brought me forth.

Please lift me from this darkness,
this anguish,
which sits deep within my soul,
within my being,
eating away at me.

Please help me.

"My child, I have heard you . . .
I know you are weary, you are tired.
I know you cannot dream.
I know you have no hope.

"For now, just rest . . .
Lean your head against me,
and surrender yourself to me.
Do not think.
Nestle yourself in my loving embrace . . .
Let it cradle you
and quiet your mind.

"Allow me this:
to be your Father, your Mother,
to be your legs and your arms,
to be your sight and your heart.
I will lift you when you cannot walk,
I will feed your soul and nourish your being.

"I know you.
You are my child, my creation.
How can the gardener not know
the flower he has planted?
You see yourself as broken.
I see you as you truly are . . .
beautiful.
You see only the dead-end alleys of your mind.
I see you . . .
full of promise,
full of life.

"*Listen* . . .
Hear your heart.
It beats with the pulse of my love.

"Hear me . . .
I have not forgotten you.
I am lifting you.

"Sit with me, my child.
Do not close your mind to me,
to life,
to grace.

Open your heart . . .
Open your arms . . .
Breathe me in . . .
Let me enter.
Let me speak with you.
Let my love encompass your entirety.
Let me wash your tears away with my touch.

"Feel my love embracing you.
Feel the showers of my grace wash away your pain.
Feel the colors of life slowly returning . . .

"I have brought you forth,
and only with my hand
shall you once again return to my Kingdom.

"You will overcome.
You will conquer.
You will see the Light within you again.

"This I promise you, for I know you.
It is not your time to go.
It is time for you to truly live and be.

"Let me envelop you with my love . . .
It will heal you.
It will calm you.
It will bring light to your heart.
It will bring joy to your steps.
You will see that life holds
an endless array of colors for you . . .

a rainbow,
full of promise,
full of divine gifts,
full of love,
full of beauty . . .
showering you with blessings
each day.

"Sit,
be,
I am here with you.
I will never leave you.
I will hold you.
Your life here still has many days and years ahead.

"Each breath you take
is my gift to you.
Behold this my child . . .
behold my light . . .
behold my grace . . .
behold my peace . . .
it is upon you.
I love you . . .
Believe this,
believe in me.
Life awaits you.

ACCEPTING AND LOVING OURSELVES

Somewhere along the journey of life, many of us forget how to love, appreciate, and accept ourselves. Instead, we may judge ourselves too harshly and lose sight of the beauty we hold. Loving and nurturing our being needs allowance, time, and true desire, and with this, we may better see ourselves in and through the eyes of God. Once we do, we will recognize how precious, how special, and how loved we are.

STONES TO USE

ROSE QUARTZ: *to promote self-love and feelings of self-worth*

OBSIDIAN: *to help break down inner blockages, to heal*

RHODONITE: *to open your heart to healing*

JADE: *to heal, to foster feelings of security*

CARNELIAN: *to protect, to empower, to support positive action toward your dreams*

FLUORITE: *to diminish the inner chatter*

TOURMALINE: *to release self-limitations as you connect to the Universe*

RUBY/GARNET: *to revitalize the spirit, to create empowerment of the self*

LAPIS LAZULI: *to see through higher wisdom*

TURQUOISE: *to connect to higher truth*

MANTRAS

"I am beautiful, as designed by God"

"I am the breath of Love"

"I am worthy"

SATNAM: *to connect to the truth within*

ONG SO HUNG: *to connect to the light within*

AAH: *to invoke confidence*

SO HUM/HAM SA: *to connect to the breath of life*

OM AH HUM: *to awaken to the Universal vibrations of the Infinite*

NAM MYOHO RENGE KYO: *to bring forth empowerment, as you connect to All*

Chant the name of the Divine, in any way that you wish

MEDITATION/VISUALIZATION

Inhale and exhale slowly. Allow your body to give in to the splendor of the quiet. See the light inside you. Envision it expanding and surrounding you. Breathe in love and exhale love. Put your hand on your heart. Feel your heart beating. Feel the beauty and preciousness that is you. Connect to the love and the joy within you. Feel and see how special you are. Believe. You are a beam of light.

Oh Beloved,
I cannot see or accept myself,
as I am.
I cannot see my beauty, my talents.
I cannot see the gifts,
the uniqueness,
the blessings You have bestowed
upon me.

My vision is blurred . . .
I see only the imperfections and flaws.
My reflection in the mirror creates
anguish in me,
and I know not how to escape it.

I am a prisoner of my mind,
of my eyes,

of negative thoughts
which whirl around in my mind,
whispering how incomplete I am.

Oh God,
help me break free of these thoughts.
Help me liberate myself
from the chains of self-doubt,
and replace them
with self-confidence
with self-esteem.

Guide me to accept myself as I am,
to see myself,
to like myself,
to know that I am worthy . . .
I am special,
I am whole.

Guide me to allow myself
the freedom to be imperfect,
as the leaf, the flower, the tree,
each having many colors and shapes,
each having great beauty . . .
all perfect in their glorious imperfections,
as created by Your divine design.

God, I want to see myself
as You have created me,
through Your eyes . . .
the eyes of Love.

I want to release my fear
and return to the seed of my soul,
to the sacred space of love,
so I may connect with You
and see the light that is acceptance.

Spirit,
I will strive to be a friend,
a loving parent, to myself.
I will caress my wounds
and embrace my being,
reminding myself
that I am worthy,
I am loved,
I am beautiful . . .
just as You made me,
just as You intended,
just as I am.

Receive me and guide me,
oh Beloved.
so that I may return
to the light that glows within me
so that I may awaken to the love
that resides within me.

With this prayer,
I sit
in Your embrace.

FOR ACCEPTANCE OF OUR LIVES

At times, our lives may not turn out the way we had envisioned, leading to disappointment and frustration. When this happens, we must remember that the Universe is always guiding our way and teaching us to honor these lessons and grow from them. By releasing our notion of what should have been, we can embrace the beauty and perfection of what is.

MANTRAS
"I trust the divine design"
"All is as it needs to be, as intended by Spirit"
"I surrender to the will of God"
"The Universe is wise"
"I am where I need to be . . . peace is with me"
SATNAM: *to connect to your higher truth*
ALLAH O AKBAR: *to trust and surrender to the will of God*
OM: *for peace*
Chant the name of the Divine, in any way that you wish

Oh Light of Lights,
I come to You,
for my life has not brought forth
what I had wished for,
what I had hoped for.

The tapestry of my life,
that which I have woven and
that which has been woven for me,
is different from what I had imagined
it would be.

God, at times,
this disappointment sits
heavily upon my heart
and confuses my mind.
And in those moments,
I forget that there is a wisdom to the Universe
beyond my understanding,
that all is for a reason,
and that You have always protected me,
and will always guide me.

Beloved,
please lead me to the depth of my core,
where truth and light reside,
so I may surrender to Your ways,
so I may embrace my life,
so I may see the colors and blessings
You have bestowed upon me.

Help me not only accept
but *celebrate* the life I have,
rejoicing in the beauty
of all its imperfections,
for they may, in fact,
be the most perfect gifts of all.

Spirit,
I will strive not only to be at peace
with that which has been placed upon my lap,
and that which I cannot change or understand,
but also to accept and honor the colors and designs

You have chosen for me—
even when they differ from
what I had expected or hoped for.

This is my intention,
upon my lips and heart,
as I embrace Your love,
yearning for peace,
for joyous acceptance
of Your divine ways.

With this,
I shall remain,
as I behold Your grace.

Amen

COPING WITH HEARTACHE
AFTER A BREAKUP

STONES TO USE

ROSE QUARTZ: *to forgive and to create healing*

MALACHITE/ONYX: *to strengthen*

CARNELIAN: *to protect and to energize*

MOSS AGATE: *to restore your spirit*

SNOW QUARTZ/GIRASOL: *to calm, to bring forth optimism*

AMBER: *to soothe your spirit*

JASPER: *to support your inner security*

RUBY/GARNET: *to revitalize, to replenish after initial healing*

MANTRAS

"I shall heal"

"My heart shall mend"

"I surrender to the will of God"

H'OPONOPONO: *to reconcile with oneself and the relationship*

LA ILLAHA ILLA HU: *to surrender to God*

Chant the name of the Divine in any way that you wish

MEDITATION/VISUALIZATION

(OPTIONAL: "FLAME MEDITATION" WITH THE USE OF A CANDLE)

Slowly breathe in and out and find your calm. Inhale peace and exhale it as such. Imagine yourself sitting under a halo of white light. Embrace this and feel the warmth of it around your heart. Feel it healing you. Imagine the sound of birds and a light breeze caressing your skin. Feel the joy of being. Believe that your heart will heal, and once again you will feel whole.

Note: please replace "him" with "her" if applicable.

Dear God,
a chapter has ended
in my life,
a chapter with
one I loved and cared for,
one I shared my deepest secrets with,
one I thought
would always be by my side,
and in my life.

My heart feels empty and shattered.
I feel tired and know not where

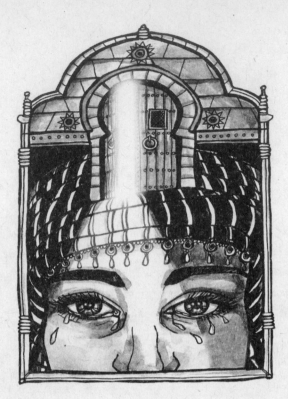

or how
to start again.

Oh Spirit,
I know You are always
protecting me,
even if I cannot comprehend the ways
of the Universe.

Please grant me strength
to not look back
and to begin my life anew.

Grant me patience,
today, tomorrow,
and in the days that follow,
to allow my body,
my mind,
and my heart to recover.

Help me find comfort
in the hope and knowledge
that my spirit will be rejuvenated,
that I will find joy again,
that I will find love again . . .

Oh God,
I wish to heal
from this heartache . . .
I wish to heal.

Today,
I will release my anger,
my resentment,
my hurt.
I will release *him*,
and wish him well.

I will give my pain
to the night winds,
and as day breaks,
I will give my tears to the clouds.
May this rainfall of tears
make flowers blossom

all around me,
once again.

I *will* release this,
and feel blessed
that I have known love.

As I embrace Your light,
oh God,
I surrender to Your will.

And with this,
I shall remain,
as I bow to Your grace.

Amen

FOR VICTIMS OF ABUSE

If you have been, or currently are, a victim of emotional, mental, phys-ical, or sexual abuse, be kind to yourself and seek help. Allow counsel-ors, social workers, and spiritual teachers to assist you. Allow yourself the time to heal. You are taking the first step in your reemergence and reawakening. Integrate positive thought and prayer into your daily life. Honor yourself and always remember that you are a child of God and thus loved beyond measure.

STONES TO USE

HEMATITE: *to ease extreme stress and anxiety*

ARAGONITE: *to open to new visions in times of heightened stress*

JASPER: *to ground you, to support feelings of security*

OBSIDIAN: *to heal, to create renewal*

CARNELIAN: *to empower, to support forward movement*

MOOKAITE: *to guide in decision making*

CALCITE: *to stimulate positive energy*

ZOISITE: *to honor, to help ease lethargy*

RUBY/GARNET: *to energize, to empower*

TOPAZ: *to strengthen body, mind, and spirit*

MALACHITE: *to strengthen the spiritual, emotional, and physical*

ONYX: *to contain emotions*

TIGER'S EYE: *to give courage*

SODALITE: *to sharpen the mind in times of high stress*

TOURMALINE: *to release self-limitations*

FLUORITE: *to diminish inner chatter and chaos*

MANTRAS

"I am the breath of Love"

"I honor myself, I am worthy"

AMMA: *to call to the Divine Mother*

NAM MYOHO RENGE KYO: *to strengthen the connection to self and the Universe, to bring forth confidence*

YA SHAFFEE O YA KHAFFEE: *to call upon the Healer*

Judaic Mantra for Fear (see appendix A)

SO HUM/HAM SA: *to connect to your inner being*

SATNAM: *to release anxiety, to connect to the Universe*

OM/SHALOM/PEACE: *to calm, to create feelings of peace*

Chant the name of the Divine, in any way that you wish

Breathe in and out slowly. Allow your mind to find its quiet and to remain silent. Feel the calm. See yourself surrounded by light. Imagine a radiant beam of healing light within you. Feel God and connect to Him. Embrace this. See a beautiful green meadow. Visualize yourself joyful and free.

Dear God,
as I lay my head upon Your door,
I feel defeated, scarred.
I have lived for too long
with this nightmare
and can no longer hide my pain.

With the passage of time,
I no longer heard my voice.
I slowly became invisible to myself.
I forgot *me*.
I was lost in another's
anger and shame.
Yet I know now,
that does not define
who I am.

Today I turn to You,
oh Spirit,
for I am ready.
Please take my hand
and guide me
with Your light . . .

I am ready
to heal.

Help me unveil my truth
and reveal to myself
what lies within my soul.
I am ready to let go of my fears
and find my freedom to *be*.
I am ready to release
this anger,
the hurt,
the misplaced shame.

Guide me,
oh Divine . . .
help me remove the layers
of pain
of unworthiness
that have weighed heavily
upon my chest,
and release them
into the ocean
of Your love . . .

Teach me to value myself,
to love myself,
to honor myself.

Lift me, oh God . . .
Help me rise
from these ashes,

so that I may find my wings
and soar into a new chapter
of my life . . .
a fulfilling one,
a joyous one,
a peaceful one.

Lead me
so that I may take steps
toward healing,
empowering myself
and fueling myself
with Your truth
each day.

Help me remember
that I am worthy and deserving
of a love that will honor
my thoughts and feelings,
that will honor
who I am.

I, too, am a child of God.
I am special,
as created by You.

With Your grace,
I will liberate my soul,
and once again . . .
I will find hope.
I will create new dreams,

and brick by brick,
I will build a sanctuary
of trust and respect.

In Your loving arms,
I will find my peace.
I will find my strength.
I will hear the song of my truth.
And I will dance into life . . .
no longer afraid.

And there . . .
I will finally *see me*.

Beloved,
I lay this prayer
upon Your gate . . .
Please receive me.

Amen

FOR VICTIMS OF A VIOLENT CRIME

We cannot comprehend the violence that is sometimes brought forth by our fellow humans. Healing from such violence is a slow process—we must allow ourselves to feel our anger, pain, and sadness. As we grieve, we will gradually walk into a place of acceptance. Allow yourself time and space, and be patient with yourself. Give your pain to God. Sit at His altar and pray for your peace.

STONES TO USE

HEMATITE: *to reduce severe anxiety and hysteria*

ARAGONITE: *to bring forth calm in times of high stress and anxiety*

CALCITE: *to heal, to allow the flow of positive energy*

AMBER: *to soothe, to lift spirits*

MALACHITE/ONYX: *to strengthen*

ROSE QUARTZ: *to forgive, to heal*

ZOISITE: *to detoxify, to honor*

RUBY: *to promote healing, reduce grief, and bring inner resolution*

GARNET: *to ease depression*

MANTRAS

"God is my anchor"

"I shall rise again"

"Light overcomes all darkness"

"Peace shall be upon me (us)"

SO HUM/HAM SA: *to connect to the seed of your soul*

HO'OPONOPONO: *to reconcile emotions within*

OM MANI PADME HUM: *to forgive*

LA ILLAHA ILLA HU: *to surrender to God*

Chant the name of the Divine, in any way that you wish

MEDITATION/VISUALIZATION

Breathe slowly and focus on your breath. Inhale and exhale until you find your calm within. Put your hand on your heart. Open your heart and ask God to hear you. Give Him your pain. See the pain releasing from your being. Imagine a healing white light within and around your body. Embrace this light. Breathe it in and out. Feel its radiant warmth healing you. Be with it. Allow it to cradle you.

Dear God,
as I kneel at the gates
of Your Heavenly Kingdom,
I feel shattered and numb,
incapable of seeing beyond my pain.

I cannot comprehend
what has happened
or why it has happened
to me (us).
I cannot understand the cruelty.
I cannot accept it.

I am scared and scarred,
I feel frozen,
incapable of being,
incapable of trusting,
incapable of opening my heart.

I cannot make sense of daily life.
I cannot sleep restfully,
as nightmares sweep into my mind . . .
reminders of an experience
I wish I could forget.

I turn to You,
oh Spirit,
as I kneel before You . . .
I give You my fears and my confusion,
my pain and my tears.
Please hear my prayer.

Lift me, oh Beloved,
for I am paralyzed
by shock and despair.
Be my legs,
so I can walk again,
with hope and belief in myself.

Be my strength,
for I feel I have
neither courage nor strength
left in me,
to face the day.

Grant me faith,
oh God.
Grant me peace . . .
hope . . .
healing.

Let the daybreak bring forth
a single ray of light,
so that I can see
and find my way home,
within myself.

Oh Spirit, in You, I trust.
Hold me . . .
I need Your embrace,
Your comfort,
Your love.

I await this,
as I rest at Your gate.
as Your broken child . . .

Dear God,
in Your loving arms
I shall find my shelter,
my refuge,
and slowly . . .
I
shall
heal.

Amen

FOR SEVERE FINANCIAL HARDSHIP

When we fall on financial hardship, we may feel vulnerable and afraid, not knowing where to turn to or what the future may hold. At such times, it is vital to remember that God has not forgotten us and that the situation can be repaired. Turn to God daily and pray. Believe. You will find the strength to take a step each day, and you shall rise once again.

STONES TO USE

CITRINE/PYRITE: *to open up the channels financially*

TIGER'S EYE: *to support positive action*

SODALITE: *to sharpen the mind, to find resolution*

TOPAZ: *to restore personal power*

MALACHITE/ONYX/TOURMALINE/JASPER: *to ground, to*
  strengthen
LAPIS LAZULI: *to see through our higher wisdom*

MANTRAS
SATNAM: *to release uncomfortable feelings and reclaim inner*
  power
NAM MYOHO RENGE KYO: *to create confidence and energize*
Judaic Mantra for Fear (see appendix A)
OM: *for peace*
Chant the name of the Divine, in any way that you wish

MEDITATION/VISUALIZATION
(OPTIONAL: "FLAME MEDITATION" WITH THE USE OF A CANDLE)
*Center yourself through your breath and find your calm. See a warm
radiant light embracing you. This is God's love. Feel this love and let it
embrace you. Visualize the many blessings you have been given. Let
this comfort you and give you peace. Envision yourself feeling secure
and take steps to rebuild your life. Know that God is with you always.
Believe.*

Dear God,
my Father, my Mother, my All,
your child has fallen . . .

I come to You,
too tired to fight,
broken, defeated,
and on my knees,
looking for strength,
for a glimpse of hope.

I feel shattered
and I know not how
to stand again.
I have lost so much.
I have lost myself.

I feel ashamed.
I feel embarrassed
to look in the mirror
and see defeat upon my face.

How did I get here,
to this place,
oh God?
And how do I recover?
How do I heal?
Where do I begin?

Spirit,
please help me to see the truth
of all there is,
of who I am.

Help me . . .
help me see
that the definition of my soul
is not in what I do,
is not in what I own . . .
that my self-worth
is not measured by wealth.

Guide me to a place
where I can find meaning,
where I can find the courage
to stand again,
where I can understand and know
that I am much more
than my material possessions.

Help me release my ego,
so I can learn from the hand of history,
from the hand of my experience,
and once again,
brick by brick,
build my life,
build a home
of truth
and grace.

I surrender to You,
oh God . . .
I believe in Your miracles,
I have faith in Your light,
and I understand
that we all need to fall at times,
so we may learn,
so we may rise
with greater humility,
strength,
and wisdom.

And I will, oh Spirit,
I *will* get up
with Your grace.

I pray and I believe
that I shall overcome this,
with Your love,
one step at a time.

This is my prayer
that I lay upon Your gate . . .
and with this,
I shall remain.

Amen

FOR THOSE DISPLACED FROM
THEIR HOMELAND

Throughout the world, many are displaced from their countries for reasons beyond their control, such as war, political unrest, or natural disasters. Often these individuals must seek refuge in another country, far from their loved ones, and often without the possibility of returning to their homes. Initially, they may face the daily challenges of integrating into a new culture and life, and they can experience various forms of unsettling feelings that may manifest in anxiety and/or depression.

In such circumstances, it is critical to understand that God is with us everywhere—not just in a specific region or area. It is also important to

remember that no one can rob us of our memories and of the love we feel
for our homeland. And in time, we may find a new love for the land
that is granting us a new beginning, a new life.

STONES TO USE

JADE: *to foster feelings of belonging, to connect to your ancestors*
    and the Universe

GIRASOL/SNOW QUARTZ (TOGETHER): *to bring forth calm*
    and optimism

CALCITE: *to heal, to create the flow of positive energy*

RUBY/GARNET: *to revitalize, to rejuvenate, to ease depression*

TURQUOISE: *to connect to our higher self*

CARNELIAN: *to empower*

MANTRAS

HO'OPONOPONO: *to reconcile, to forgive*

MAA BA AAH: *to foster feelings of belonging as we connect to the*
    seed of our soul and the Universe

Chant the name of the Divine, in any way that you wish

Oh Beloved,
I come to You feeling alone,
in a place so distant . . .
so far from my roots.

I never knew I could feel
such a pain within my heart . . .
a loss,
a yearning,
for that which no longer is,

for a land and a people
that have been taken from me.

As the sun rises and sets each day,
as the moon glistens in the dark skies,
I long for the hills and valleys,
the rivers and plains,
the alleys and streets . . .

I long for the faces I once knew,
for those I love . . .
for the familiar fragrances
that would awaken my senses . . .
for the ground that I walked upon,
and the rich soil that would
caress my bare feet.

I am lost in time,
in the hallways of yesterdays.
I sleep with the memories
of a life far gone,
and in the midst of the night,
before dawn's break,
I awake with a thirst
that cannot be quenched.

I live each day as a stranger,
isolated,
with no one to call my own . . .
in a different world,

in a distant reality,
grieving the loss of a life
that no longer is.

Oh Beloved,
help me stand again,
help me understand,
help me forgive this hand of fate
that has torn me from all I knew,
that has torn the pages of my story . . .

Help me, dear God . . .
help me open my heart
to new experiences,
to a new people.

God,
I am grateful for this new land,
this gracious place,
that has allowed me refuge,
as I try to find my footing.

Help me see
the beauty of the vast terrain before me,
and in it,
find a comfort,
a knowing
that I have come to this place
for You have willed it for me . . .

Help me see that I will not lose myself,
that I will not lose my memories,
for those are my treasures.

Show me how
to walk on this path,
to embark upon this journey,
with ease.

Guide me
so I may write a new story,
begin a new chapter,
so I may build once again . . .
a life, a home,
that I shall cherish.

With Your grace,
I shall rise.

Shokran

CIRCLE OF PRAYER FOR
COUNTRIES WITH UNREST

*During turbulent times in the world, we can create a synergy of posi-
tive thought and vibration through prayer. Recite this prayer alone or in
a group.*

Passages of this prayer can be recited in a rhythmic pattern by a
    group, to bring forth greater strength and empowerment.
"Lead us to Your grace"
"Lead us to peace"
"May peace prevail always"
Chant the name of the Divine, in any way that you wish

MEDITATION/VISUALIZATION

Inhale and exhale light and peace. In your heart and your mind's eye, hold the people and region of the world you are concentrating on in white light.

Dear God,
as we close our eyes
and open our hearts in prayer,
we turn to You.

Oh God,
please hear our voices.

We pray for the people of [name the country],
who live in turbulence and uncertainty
each day.

May Your grace and blessing of peace
unfold unto this nation
in the weeks ahead,
and may its people be enveloped
by Your light.

May these dark times lift,
and may the sun pour in,
with a promise of hope.

As they fear for their lives,
may they be protected by Your grace,
and may their homes
be havens of safety and peace.

May their bodies be shielded from harm,
may their spirits hold strong,
and may they not lose faith.

May the sea of Your infinite love
wash away all hatred and anger.

Dear God,
with Your grace and mercy,
may the rains wash away all bloodshed,
all violence,
from this sacred land.

We mourn those who have lost their lives.
May their families know
that the world is praying for them,
and may faith be their anchor.

We pray from the purest place within,
that the young men and women,
the elders,

the children of this nation,
be protected beneath the veil of Your love.

Dear Spirit,
as we turn to You,
let the winds of change bring forth
freedom and harmony.

Let the voice of Truth ring across the land
and herald a new era of promise and peace.

May the sounds of joy
and rays of Your light
soon be upon this nation.

This is our prayer,
our plea,
our wish,
and our deepest hope.

Amen

FOR A COMMUNITY IN CRISIS:
WE SHALL HEAL

In the wake of tragedy, we can unite in our grief as a people of one nation, of one world, to bring forth healing. We sit devastated, paralyzed by shock and disbelief, not comprehending how or why this could have happened. For today and the days that lie ahead, let us turn to God to guide our way on and strengthen us. Let us turn to prayer, to the divine beam of light that resides within us. This is how we can begin to heal, as one heart, in unison, with one voice . . . being light, spreading love and hope.

MANTRAS
"We shall heal"
"We are the breath of Love"
"We are the children of Light"
"God is with me. Faith is my anchor"
Chant the name of the Divine, in any way that you wish

MEDITATION/VISUALIZATION
(OPTIONAL: "FLAME MEDITATION" WITH THE USE OF A CANDLE)
Meditate and visualize a healing white light within and all around Spread this to your home and neighborhood, to cities near and far, to other countries, and, finally, to the whole earth. In your mind's eye, bring forth this peace and light, and direct it to the families who have lost their loved ones, and to those who have lost their lives.

Dear God,
we turn to You to help us
in this most harrowing of hours.

As we sit with You,
our hearts are full of pain and anguish.
In utter shock and disbelief,
we cannot shake this agonizing darkness.

Please,
help us see the dawn,
the light within,
and spread it throughout the land,
as a sea of love and hope.

Help us be a shoulder to cry on,
to lean on,
for those who have lost their loved ones
so tragically.

We pray for their peace.
We pray for their faith.
We pray for their strength.
Please let them know they are not alone.

Spirit,
please grant peace
to those whose journey here
has ended in violence.

Let them know
as they leave this earthly plane
that they were loved,
that their lives were valued,
that their legacy will live on,
as we honor them,
forever,
each day.

They will never be forgotten,
and they will be our angels of Light.
And through their light,
we will lead this nation
to a place of peace and hope.

With Your grace,
we will heal,
we will find peace,
we will dissolve our anger,
and once again
we will emerge,
stronger,
as a people,
hand in hand,
walking side by side.

This is our prayer.
This is our hope.

Lead us,
God,
with Your grace,
and we shall follow.

Amen

hand of fate

One of my dearest students of twenty years had a disability that he had been struggling with for most of his life. When he was seven years old, he went through a sliding glass door that his mother had just closed. This accident caused him to lose a portion of his right hand, limiting its use. This incident, which had seldom been discussed between him and his mother, was buried deep in his memories.

For the first seventeen years I knew him, he struggled with this disability. He was angry and ashamed, and had never truly healed emotionally from the accident, which had, in his mind, scarred his life. This anguish, coupled with his dramatic personality, often fueled him with an intensity that made him feel overly restless and reactive, and therefore difficult to deal with in relationships. I believe he fought this battle with himself for years and would find small escapes in the dramatic exits and entrances of so many in his life. Although he still had many friends, his closest bond was with his beloved dog, Sammie, a playful mutt he had rescued from a shelter several years back.

For the longest time, he would come to me for my guidance,

and I would counsel him on career and personal matters. I could see the tides he would emotionally undergo, crashing deeply into feelings of frustration and pain. I knew he needed to forgive his mother and the hand of fate for the accident in order to truly heal. But I also knew he had to come into this realization on his own.

As Sammie aged and got ill, I assumed he would spiral downward into darkness and despair. Sammie was his best friend, and facing the loss would be a challenge to his already wounded soul. However, as he faced the passing of his dog, he began to confront his own aging, his mortality. And this process brought forth an inner awakening to the knowledge that our days are numbered and that life itself is a gift to be enjoyed and cherished. In this realization, he understood that he needed to heal his inner wounds. And so he began to attend more of my classes, with a renewed interest in growing, learning, and showing up in his own life. I knew it was just a matter of time before he would resolve his feelings about the accident with his mother and create healing.

Indeed, soon after he lost his dog, his mother became gravely ill, and he came to the realization that time was precious and he needed to resolve this old wound, which had occurred fifty years before. During one of his final visits with his mother, as she lay in her hospital bed, she brought up the accident and asked him for his forgiveness. Her honest yearning for resolution opened his heart to the act of forgiveness.

And *in that moment*, as he forgave his mother—and the hand of fate—he was awakened to the Light within him and the dark clouds lifted from his being. No longer feeling victimized, he experienced a rebirth, and a new path was illuminated before him.

With this pivotal realization, an amazing awakening occurred at a core level. And this is where I was—and still am—in awe of him.

He began to excel at his work, embracing the challenges with a newfound confidence; he was further recognized for his public work in front of a huge crowd at a historical LA landmark. I was blessed to be there that starry night and see the transformation that had taken place. It was not only remarkable, but also humbling to witness. As he spoke, he exuded joy and confidence—his hand was no longer his focal point. He was finally free; he was charming and radiant, and he captivated everyone's hearts. And as he continued his spiritual journey, disciplined and committed, he became a joyful presence at all my classes and returned to a more steady practice of yoga.

He also learned to embrace the quiet of the night. He had always been afraid of nightfall and could not stand the stillness of a quiet home. But now, reawakened to himself, he would sit at night in the single-candle ambience of his home and embrace the silence that would unfold in and around him—the miraculous silence of prayer and meditation.

His celebration of a renewed life concluded with having a striking ornate tattoo carved into his right arm, symbolizing his acceptance, his liberation, and his peace. His hand of fate had presented his single biggest life challenge—and the one that would ultimately bring about his greatest awakening.

prayers for illness and loss

ACCEPTING AND HONORING
THE AGING OF A PARENT

Witnessing the aging of our parents can be a very difficult emotional journey, for it is a reminder of the inevitable: their passing. In time, we can come to terms with this by reminding ourselves that the spirit never dies. Even when our parents transition to the spirit world, they will always remain with us.

Note: please replace "she, "her," and "mother" with
"he," "him," and "father" if applicable.

MANTRAS
"I surrender to Thy will"
"I trust the divine design"
"Life continues, love continues, spirits never die"
OM: *for peace*
SATANAMA: *to connect to the cycle of life*

God of light,
I sit and watch my parent each day,
as she is becoming less able,
more vulnerable,
walking closer
to the seed of her soul,
to the child that resides in her core.

With each declining moment
of her mind and body,
I see her struggle . . .

I see her accepting
that which she can no longer do,
that which she can no longer change.

Spirit,
I know I cannot
stop the hands of time,
that I cannot stop the passing of
the days, nights,
and seasons,
but it pains my heart
to see her weaken
and become more forgetful,
with each passing moment.

In my mind's eye,
I thought she would
always remain
the mother of my early youth.
I never imagined her frail,
incapable of doing
the small things of everyday life.

It is hard to see this . . .
and each time I do,
my heart grieves a little,
as I know what lies ahead.

I know that her spirit
is slowly preparing

to depart from this earthly womb,
to enter Your embrace.

I turn to You,
oh Spirit,
for I know not how to prepare for this.
I know not how to move through
the tides of deep sadness,
of deep loneliness.

Guide me to the acceptance
that my parent is coming full circle,
slowly getting ready
to take her final rest.

Guide me to the knowledge
that spirit never dies . . .
that as she rests,
she will find peace,
and no longer struggle
with her earthly aches, pains, and losses.
And there, she will reunite
with her loved ones,
in a joy so deep.

God, lead me
to trust that one day,
when my time has come,
I will join her in Your Heavenly Skies,
and forever be . . .

Until that day,
I ask You, oh Spirit,
to grant me courage and fortitude
to bring her happiness, comfort, and love
to fuel her with security,
to fuel her with peace,
for the remainder of her days.

With this,
I shall remain,
upon Your altar,
and with this,
I shall find the strength,
to go through this passage
of life.

God,
I bow to Your grace.

FOR ONE WHO LIVES WITH PHYSICAL PAIN EACH DAY

Millions of people throughout the world live with chronic physical pain. This reality can be very trying and challenging to the soul and in time can deplete physical and emotional stamina. Seeking the help of health practitioners, receiving support from family and friends, and creating sacred space each day can bring tremendous comfort and love to the body, mind, and spirit.

STONES TO USE

(*Initially use lightly to see how your body reacts.*)

CARNELIAN: *to protect, to energize*

ZOISITE: *to help with lethargy and exhaustion*

CALCITE: *to create healing*

GIRASOL: *to bring forth optimism*

SODALITE: *to support health and well-being*

TOPAZ: *to strengthen when depleted*

MALACHITE/ONYX/TOPAZ/TOURMALINE: *to strengthen*

GARNET/RUBY: *to revitalize, to rejuvenate*

MANTRAS

"I am the breath of Love"

"I am whole, I am love"

*Mangala Charan Mantra (see appendix A): to surrender to the
    wisdom of the Universe*

OM HANSAM HANSAHA: *for good health and its protection*

SO HUM/HAM SA: *to connect to the breath and find its peace and
    wholeness*

OM TARE TUTTARE TURE SOHA: *to remove emotional,
    mental, or physical obstacles*

MEDITATION/VISUALIZATION

*Take deep inhalations and exhalations, concentrating on your
breath until you feel a calm within you. Visualize a healing golden light
around the area of your pain. Feel its warm radiance penetrate into your
pain and dissolve it. Breathe in this energy of healing into your body.*

Mother Divine,
I come to You with a wish,

with a prayer upon my heart,
for I have lived too long
with this pain.

I sleep and awaken with it.
Pain is my constant companion.
Its walls close around me,
making my world smaller,
encompassing my entire being,
holding me tight,
from dusk to dawn,
awake or in slumber,
never letting me go . . .
It leaves me with no room for wonder,
for hope,
for laughter,
or desire . . .

Pain remains with me in each breath,
grasping at me with each inhale and exhale . . .
a constant presence . . .
one that I cannot bear any longer,
one that makes me question
my sanity, my strength,
one that I cannot seem to escape . . .

Oh Mother, help me.
I wish to live a life
free of this constant anguish.
I wish to be liberated
from this bondage.

Give me strength
to break the walls of fear,
of darkness,
of despair.

Lead me
to fill my body
with light,
with calm,
with a healing peace.

Oh Mother Divine,
I know You are with me
each day.
I know You are the one
who embraces me,
who anchors me.

I kneel to You,
in Your light,
asking You
to please receive this prayer . . .
please help me heal.

This is my hope,
my wish,
the prayer within my soul.

And with Your grace,
I shall remain.

Amen

FOR ONE WITH DEPRESSION

Depression is an illness and nothing to be ashamed of or to hide. Please honor yourself by seeking help and allowing healing of the mind, body, and spirit. Remember to be patient, nonjudgmental, and loving to yourself at all times.

STONES TO USE

GARNET/RUBY: *to energize and enhance your spirit, self-esteem, and vitality*

GIRASOL/SNOW QUARTZ (TOGETHER): *to calm, to bring forth hope and optimism*

ROSE QUARTZ: *to foster empowerment and self-love*

CARNELIAN: *to honor the self*

MALACHITE: *to strengthen, to align the emotional, spiritual, and physical*

JADE/JASPER: *to promote security*

MANTRAS

"I believe in me"

"I am not this, I am love"

"I am a being of light, joy is within me"

"I am the breath of Love"

YA SHAFFEE O YA KHAFFEE: *to call upon God for healing*

ONG SO HUNG: *to open yourself, to the light within you*

OM HANSAM HANSAHA: *for health protection*

SATNAM: *to connect to the light within*

OM TARE TUTTARE TURE SOHA: *to remove emotional, mental, or physical obstacles*

NAM MYOHO RENGE KYO: *to rejuvenate the self, to bring forth inner confidence*

Chant the name of the Divine, in any way that you wish

MEDITATION/VISUALIZATION

(OPTIONAL: "FLAME MEDITATION" WITH THE USE OF A CANDLE)

(RECOMMENDED ADDITION: "WALKING MEDITATION")

Inhale and exhale self-love. Inhale and exhale peace and joy. Imagine yourself surrounded by flowers and light. Hear the sound of a brook or river, and feel it calming your senses. See yourself basking in this splendor. Put your hand on your heart. See the light within you, as it emanates and extends all around you with its warm radiance, healing your mind and heart. As you envision this, see yourself finding joy, belief, and hope. Believe . . . believe . . . you will find your healing.

Oh Spirit,
I sit in the darkness
of the walls within me,
unable to breathe,
unable to find the light within . . .

A hollow, empty feeling
fills my body,
which I can barely
find strength to overcome.

I seek refuge in sleep,
but despair,
hopelessness,
and the ebb and flow of this grayness,
leave me not,
and fill the hallways of my mind . . .

I struggle to find my voice,
to find the joy,

the colors,
that will lift me
from this deep pain and anguish.

God, I turn to You . . .
I wish to break through
to overcome these tides,
to see the walls collapse,
to see the light emerge,
to see my spirit lifted
into a blissful peace.

Please, oh Spirit,
lead me to those who can
help me heal my heart,
heal my mind.

Lead me to those who can
help me find my wings,
so I may take flight
into the joy of daily life,
so I may find hope
and belief.

God,
I know that this darkness
does not define me.
I must believe that it shall pass.
and that I will find my healing.

In Your loving embrace
I shall find my rest.
And as I awaken,
to the birth of a new day,
may I find the faith to know . . .
that I *can* find lightness of being,
that I *can* find joy,
that I *can* find my voice
once again.

With this,
I shall breathe,
I shall believe,
I shall remain.

Beloved,
please receive
my prayer,
as I sit at Your door.

Shokran . . . Amen

CONFRONTING AND RELEASING ADDICTION

It is not an easy task to look at our lives truthfully and see all our challenges. This requires not only courage and faith but also the desire to let go of patterns that do not serve us. Claiming our lives once again can be arduous but will lead to the liberation of the self. As we allow ourselves to experience the discomfort of letting go and open ourselves to recovery, we slowly get a glimpse of out true self, which is beyond beautiful.

STONES TO USE

ZOISITE: *to detoxify*

RHODONITE/OBSIDIAN: *to remove blockages*

CALCITE: *to cleanse, to clear the body*

JADE: *to bring forth security, to protect, to heal*

CARNELIAN: *to honor the self*

GIRASOL: *to empower, to bring forth joy*

MOSS AGATE: *to restore*

MALACHITE: *to align body, mind, and spirit*

ROSE QUARTZ: *to promote self-love*

JASPER/TOURMALINE/MALACHITE/ONYX: *to ground, to strengthen*

MANTRAS

"I am the breath of Love"

"I am not of fear, but of Love"

"I am worthy"

SO HUM/HAM SA: *to connect to the breath of life*

OM HANSAM HANSAHA: *to promote good health*

OM TARE TUTTARE TURE SOHA: *to assist in removal of physical, mental, or emotional blockages, to bring forth inner peace*

Gayatri Mantra (see appendix A)

Judaic Mantra for Fear (see appendix A)

Chant the name of the Divine, in any way that you wish

Through your breath, find your calm. As you inhale and exhale love, see yourself surrounded by a golden white light. Envision yourself healthy, healed, and joyous. Repeat this daily as many times as you wish, until you find your serenity.

Oh Father Divine,
I turn to You,
from the deepest place within me,
for I know You will not judge
how scared I feel,
how broken I am.

Today,
I know I cannot lie to myself any longer.
My soul is crying,
screaming . . .
I cannot ignore it.

I do not want to believe it.
I do not want to speak about it.
I do not wish to reveal the truth.

I have hidden myself,
and have hidden *from* myself,
under the veil of lies and deception.
I have lost my loved ones.
I have lied to them.
I have distanced myself from them.

This is not me.
This is not the life I wanted.

I try each day,
not to give into temptation,
not to allow the shadow to get too close.
I try, God, I try . . .
But my will is not enough.

Oh God, please help me . . .
I no longer want to live in shame and pain,
and yet
I do not want to die.
I do not want to drown.

Please lift me from the depth
of these tumultuous waters,
so I may breathe once again.

Help me, Spirit . . .
I want to feel the warmth of the sun
penetrate through my being.
I want to see the shore of life,
of dreams and possibilities.
I want to remember that I am worthy,
that I am loved.

Help me wash away my guilt,
my shame.
Help me understand my pain.
Help me understand myself.

I kneel to You,
oh God.
I am struggling within myself
each minute of each day.
I am frightened
by what I need to face,
by the step I must take
to surrender.

I turn to You,
for I know . . .
only You can help me find
the truth of me
behind these walls of fear.
Only You can help me walk,
until *I* learn to walk again.
Only You can help me live,
until *I* learn to live again.

From this darkness
to Your light . . .
I surrender to You.
Let it be, oh God . . .
let it be.

Amen

FOR ONE WITH A SERIOUS ILLNESS

When faced with a serious illness, we need patience and faith, as well as support from our loved ones, to overcome our feelings of loss and fear. Sitting with God will give us the strength to withstand the challenges that illness can bring.

STONES TO USE
Please refer to the "Stone Healing" section on page 344 for more information on stone usage during illness.

MANTRAS
YA SHAFFEE O YA KHAFFEE: *for healing*

ONG SO HUNG: *to see the light within*

SO HUM / HAM SA: *to connect to the breath of life*

OM TARE TUTTARE TURE SOHA: *to assist in the removal of mental, physical, or emotional obstacles*

OM HANSAM HANSAHA: *for health protection*

SATNAM: *to connect to your higher truth*

Chant the name of the Divine, in any way that you wish

Dear God,
my soul is screaming,
in the quiet of the night.
I feel so scared,
frightened
beyond what I could
ever imagine.

How can I face this illness,
which is depleting me?

Where can I find
the strength, the faith, the reserve?

Oh God,
how did this happen to me,
and why?

There are no answers,
yet I have so many questions.
There are no certainties,
no promises,
but I am in need of a promise
to hold on to,
a pillar to lean on,
a ray of hope to believe in.

Oh God,
I feel sick in my fear.
I feel so overwhelmed.
Please help me,
as I turn to You . . .

I want to be alive,
to heal,
to be healthy.
Please strengthen me.

I am leaning on the wings
of Your angels.
I am praying with all I am . . .
hoping, wishing,

for my body to find release
from this illness.

Grant me the fortitude,
the wisdom,
the patience,
to withstand this storm . . .
to confront this,
to accept this,
and to see the warmth of the sun
upon me once again.

Grace me oh God,
with peace of being.
Help me let go of earthly limitations,
so I may embrace the moment
and find joy in the *now*.

Beloved,
I know You have never left me . . .
You have always loved me . . .
I will let *this*
be my anchor.

I will remember
that I am not this illness
but Your child,
Your creation of light.

I am not this fear
but Your love.

God,
as I sit at Your door,
I know I will be okay,
for I shall remain
in Your embrace . . .
always.

Amen

FOR A LOVED ONE WHO IS ILL

When our loved ones fall ill, they are in need of our love and support. Prayer can anchor us at these trying times.

MANTRAS
YA SHAFFEE O YA KHAFFEE: *to call upon the Divine for healing*
OM: *to help center you, to neutralize your energy field*
Chant the name of the Divine, in any way that you wish

MEDITATION/VISUALIZATION
(OPTIONAL: "FLAME MEDITATION" WITH THE USE OF A CANDLE)
Inhale and exhale each breath slowly. Center yourself and find your calm. Imagine a golden healing light around your loved one. See its radiance penetrating through his/her body.

Note: please replace "he" and "him" with
"she" and "her" if applicable.

Oh Divine Light,
I kneel before You,
as I come in deepest prayer,
for my loved one is ill.

Dear God,
wash away this illness
in Your holy waters
of grace and love.

Please lift him,
so he can regain his health,
so he can become whole again,
so he can live his life fully.

Surround him with Your light,
oh Beloved.
Heal him,
from the wounds
within his body.

Guide him
to courage,
to strength,
to the pathways of healing.

Oh Beloved,
I bow to You in prayer
Please hear me,
and with Your divine grace,

deliver my loved one
to recovery and health.

This is the prayer within my heart,
and with this,
I sit.

Amen . . . Shokran

FOR SURGERY

Before surgery, our minds may wander to a place of anxiety and fear.
At such times, we can find peace and comfort by anchoring ourselves in
faith, relinquishing control, and putting ourselves in God's hands.
Surrender yourself to God.

STONES TO USE
(See appendix B for specific areas.)
MALACHITE/ONYX: *to strengthen oneself before and/or after*
surgery
HEMATITE: *to energize the physical body before and/or after*
surgery, to reduce anxiety
BLOODSTONE: *to help with blood-related issues before and/or*
after surgery
ZOISITE: *to help minimize lethargy after surgery*
RUBY/GARNET: *to energize oneself after surgery, once the*
healing process has begun

MANTRAS

Judaic Mantra for Fear (see appendix A)

YA SHAFFEE O YA KHAFFEE: *to call upon God, the Healer*

OM HANSAM HANSAHA: *for health protection*

NAM MYOHO RENGE KYO: *to strengthen the body, mind, and spirit and connect to the Universe after surgery*

"Peace is with me"

"I sit in Your embrace"

"Faith is my anchor"

OM: *for peace*

SATNAM: *to release anxiety, to find the confidence within*

SO HUM/HAM SA: *to connect to the breath of being*

MEDITATION/VISUALIZATION

Take deep breaths and quiet your mind. Imagine a healing golden light within and all around you. Focus on the area of your body where the procedure will take place. Inhale and exhale peace and strength to it. See and feel it healing.

Dear God,
I come to You,
as I await my surgery.

Please bless my body and spirit.
Open the channels
to my healing . . .
Help me release
my fears and trepidations,
and replace them
with the hope of,

and belief in,
well-being.

Bless me with Your light,
oh God,
as I go into deep sleep . . .
Protect my body,
so it may receive
the gift of good health.

May the hands of Your grace
guide this surgery
and the healing touch of my doctors.

May you lead them to mend
the brokenness,
the wound within my body,
so I may be strengthened
and whole again.

May I awaken with
a calm and hopeful spirit,
anchored in faith.

God,
I am in Your hands . . .
this I trust
with all I am.

Bless me with Your light,
as I sit . . .
embracing hope and healing.

Amen

FOR ONE WHO IS TERMINALLY ILL

*Having a terminal illness and facing mortality can be extremely diffi-
cult and is a journey of many steps. We must trust and surrender to
God, and remember that this passage of life will lead to the next. Death
of the physical self is not the end, but a transition, as spirit never dies.*

MANTRAS

"*I surrender to Thy will*"

"*I am love and as such I will remain*"

"*Peace be with me, peace be upon me*"

SO HUM/HAM SA: *to connect deeper to your soul and to the
essence of God*

Mangala Charan Mantra (see appendix A)

ONG SO HUNG: *to connect to your inner light*

SATNAM: *to release uncomfortable feelings, to be with your
higher truth*

LA ILLAHA ILLA HU: *to recognize that the only truth is God*

The Lord's Prayer (see appendix A)

TAT TVAM ASI: *to see the whole*

WAKAN TANKA: *to connect to the mystery of life*

Chant the name of the Divine, in any way that you wish

(OPTIONAL: "FLAME MEDITATION" WITH THE USE OF A CANDLE)

See yourself as a beam of light. Imagine the child within you, and allow this child to laugh and feel joyous in a field of green. Envision yourself immersed in light. See yourself dancing in it, freely, joyously, and peacefully. See your loved ones in the spirit world. See yourself embracing them. Feel the joy. Feel the love. Feel the peace.

Dear God,
I am weary and unwell.
The weight of my illness
has exceeded what my body can endure.
I feel my journey here is almost complete.

The time is almost upon me
to surrender,
to release all earthly attachments,
to welcome the next chapter . . .

Oh God, at times,
I am scared of what may lie ahead . . .
of how to relinquish my earthly life,
and find the courage to face the journey ahead.
In moments of such fear,
I feel like a child
in need of a loving embrace.

Yet I know . . .
I know You are with me.
I know I am not alone.
I feel You . . .

I feel Your loving arms
holding me close.
I trust this.

Dear God,
I know You will soon call me to join You
in Your Heavenly Skies.

You will carry me on
the wings of Your angels.
I know there . . .
I will be at peace.

I am returning home . . .
returning to Your embrace.
Forever,
I am Your child.

Please, dear God,
help my family and friends
find their peace
in letting me go.

Help them remember
that I will never truly leave them,
that my spirit and love
will be with them,
always.

I know my loved ones await me,
and when I cross over to Your Heavenly Skies,

I will unite with them once again.
In much anticipated joy and peace,
I shall embrace them.

Dear God,
grace me with Your love,
lift me in Your divine light,
so I may journey through this final road
with ease and grace.

I am ready for my final rest.
Please receive me.

Amen

FOR A DYING CHILD

The pain we endure in life can at times be unimaginable. Losing a child is heart wrenching and often beyond the scope of what the mind can grasp. At such moments, may God grant you with strength, faith, and, above all, peace in the knowledge that love never dies, and that the spirit of your child will always live on.

STONES TO USE (FOR THE PARENT)

ARAGONITE/HEMATITE: *to bring relief in times of severe anxiety*

TOPAZ/MALACHITE/ONYX/TOURMALINE: *to ground, to strengthen*

SNOW QUARTZ: *to bring forth calm*
JADE: *to foster feelings of security within you*

MANTRA
Chant the name of the Divine, in any way that you wish

MEDITATION/VISUALIZATION
(OPTIONAL: "FLAME MEDITATION" WITH THE USE OF A CANDLE)
Slowly breathe in and out, until you have reached a state of calm within. Visualize a white light all around your child. Imagine her smiling peacefully. Put your hand on your heart, and feel God's love and her peace.

Note: please replace "she," "her," and "mother" with "he," "him," and "father" if applicable.

Dear God,
I turn to You,
for my pain is beyond measure.
I am losing my child . . .
the most cherished part of me.

I know not how to endure this.
I know not how to stop my heart from bleeding.
I know not how to find the strength to face this,
to let her go.

I am not prepared for this.
Nothing will ever be the same again.

Oh God,
please grant me courage . . .
courage to know that I will survive this,
that I will find strength I cannot find today,
that I will once again,
find a will to live.

God, please grant me faith . . .
faith to know that in each step,
in each turn,
You are with me . . .
faith to know that one day,
I will reunite with my child
in Your Heavenly Skies.

God, please grant me patience . . .
patience to hold Your hand
as You lead me,
so that I may continue my journey here
with purpose and meaning,
honoring my child and her legacy
each day.

I will always carry her
in my heart and my life.
I will always love her,
beyond measure,
beyond time . . .

Help me, God.
Help me let her go for now,
so that she may be at peace.

Let her know that Your love
will be my anchor and strength
as I continue my journey here.

Oh God,
I pray for my child . . .

Help her release her suffering.
Let my tears wash away her pain,
as she surrenders her earthly body.
May her final moments on Earth be of peace.

Send Your angels
from the Heavens to her,
as You lift her spirit
with Your grace.
Help her to not be afraid,
as she transitions into Your Eternal Embrace.
Help her cross over to You in calm
and with dignity.

Oh Lord,
I hold on to Thee,
with all I am . . .
please receive this,
my deepest prayer.

This I ask with a heart full of a mother's love.

Amen

〜

GRIEVING FOR A LOVED ONE

Losing a loved one may feel beyond what the human heart can endure. As our hearts break, only love, support, time, and faith can help us get through this most trying of periods. Prayer is key to grieving, for it is in this sacred space that we can cry, wail, get angry, and express our innermost pain without feeling judged. And through this process, we can reach acceptance and peace, and, eventually, find joy in the remembrance of our loved ones. May those who are grieving truly allow themselves the space and time to heal.

STONES TO USE

ARAGONITE/HEMATITE: *to bring calm in times of high stress and anxiety*

JASPER: *to help give strength, to ground*

JADE: *to support healing and security*

MALACHITE/ONYX TOPAZ/TOURMALINE: *to strengthen, to contain our emotions*

RHODONITE: *to heal in matters of the heart*

MOSS AGATE OR SNOW QUARTZ: *to heal, to restore*

ZOISITE: *to help with exhaustion and lethargy*

RUBY OR GARNET: *to energize, to help bring forth renewal in the latter stages of grieving*

GIRASOL: *to bring forth hope and optimism, in the latter stages of grieving*

MANTRAS

"I surrender to Thy will"

"Faith is my anchor, God is my strength"

SO HUM / HAM SA: *to connect to the breath of life and the essence of God*

LA ILLAHA ILLA HU: *to recognize that the only truth is God*

The Lord's Prayer (see appendix A)

Chant the name of the Divine, in any way that you wish

MEDITATION/VISUALIZATION

(OPTIONAL: "FLAME MEDITATION" WITH THE USE OF A CANDLE)

Listen to your breath and find your quiet. See the light around you, connecting you to your loved one. There, in this space of peace, speak to your loved one. Feel the love you shared and let it comfort you. It will always remain.

Please note that it may take time to be able to chant a mantra or do meditation/visualization. Be kind and loving to yourself and ease into these practices.

Note: please replace "he" and "him" with "she" and "her" if applicable.

Dear God,
in these unbearable moments of grief,
I turn to You,
for it is only You
who can grant me peace
and help me heal.

I feel that my despair is beyond
what my soul can bear.
I feel that my heart has broken,
has been shattered.

Oh God, grant me strength to hold on,
for I feel lost, weak,
and incapable of seeing
beyond this hour of darkness.

Grant me patience,
as I walk through this haze,
clinging on to my sanity.

Lift me into a stream of light,
where I can find a way
to make peace with this pain.

Grant me faith,
and help me accept Your ways,
although I cannot always understand
or see them clearly.

Dear Lord,
grant me the vision to see
that You always love us.
May Your love be my anchor,
as my soul sways
in the winds of uncertainty.

Grant me the wisdom to know
that our spirits never die,
and that one day,
we will all reunite.

I pray that as time passes,
this pain will dissolve
and my heart will slowly mend.

I will always honor my loved one
and our memories.
My love for him will be
my forever-treasure.

Dear Lord, bless him,
as he has come
into Your arms.

I pray that he is at peace and resting
in Your Heavenly Skies.

God,
with Your grace,
I sit.
Please . . .
receive my prayer.

Amen

COPING WITH THE LOSS OF A SPOUSE

The passing of a life partner can be excruciatingly difficult to endure, as we are forced to face a life void of his or her physical presence. Seeking the help of grief counselors and bereavement support groups can be invaluable to our healing during this time and can also allow remind us that we are not alone.

Time is needed to transition from deep grief into acceptance, to understand that our loved one is always with us and that we may slowly shift our earthly relationship with them to a spiritual one.

STONES TO USE

HEMATITE/ARAGONITE: *to relieve severe anxiety, to bring forth calm*

AMBER: *to lift the spirits*

GARNET/RUBY: *to ease depression, to revitalize, to re-energize*

GIRASOL: *to bring forth hope after initial period of grieving*

ONYX OR MALACHITE: *to strengthen reserves*

SNOW QUARTZ: *to calm*

ZOISITE: *to relieve exhaustion and lethargy*

SODALITE: *to sharpen the mind*

MANTRAS

"Spirit lives on, love lives on"

SO HUM/HAM SA: *to connect to the breath of life*

SATNAM: *to embrace the essence of our being*

Mangala Charan Mantra (see appendix A):
    to surrender to the wisdom of the Universe

Chant the name of the Divine, in any way that you wish

Light two white candles, one for yourself and one for your spouse. Breathe, each time inhaling and exhaling deeper. Close your eyes and sit in the quiet of your being. Envision your spouse and yourself surrounded by a beautiful white light, in a loving embrace. Let it cradle you.

*Note: please replace "he" and "him" with
"she" and "her" if applicable.*

My dearest God,
God of here and there,
of vastness beyond . . .
my heart is broken
and my body fatigued,
beaten down,
by my deep grief.

Oh Spirit,
my beautiful [name of spouse]
is no longer here . . .

I miss him so,
and cannot imagine a life
without him by my side.
God, how can it be
that the sun shall rise and set,
and the moon appear each night,
without him here
to witness their glory with me?

How can I count the stars without him?
How can I sleep without holding his hand?
With whom will I laugh?
With whom will I cry?

I can feel his comforting presence
all around me.
I can hear his voice at times
and see his face . . .

I visit my memories with him . . .
the years of togetherness,
the years of building a home, a life.

I feel his imprint on everything I touch,
on everything I see . . .
I will live his legacy
through each breath I take.
I will live this life for him and myself,
for the remainder of my days.

Grant me faith,
oh Spirit,
to understand my grief,
to understand that I have not truly lost him,
for he is still with me.

Grant me strength
to walk the rest of my days
with a peace, a knowing
that one day . . .

we will reunite.
And there . . .
where angels of love
and birds of song reside,
where God sits on the throne of life,
he and I will meet again.

And when we do,
all longing will dissolve
into a sea of infinite grace.

Until then,
Beloved,
I pray that he is at peace,
cradled in Your loving embrace.

I pray to always connect
with him . . .
my guiding angel.

I pray to heal from this grief
and once again
feel alive,
and live this life,
for him and I.

With Your grace,
I sit.

Amen

FOR RENEWAL AFTER A MISCARRIAGE

Pregnancy is a sacred time in a woman's life, and an unexpected miscarriage can cause devastation, grief, and emptiness. Allow time to grieve for your loss, and trust that nature always guides us to healing. With time, your spirit and body will replenish. Be patient with yourself and the process. Know and believe that you will find peace once again.

STONES TO USE

BLOODSTONE: *to balance hormones and blood flow*

ZOISITE: *to ease lethargy*

RUBY/GARNET: *to energize, to revitalize, to ease depression*

MOSS AGATE: *to restore the spirit*

SNOW QUARTZ/GIRASOL (USED TOGETHER): *to calm, to bring forth optimism*

CARNELIAN: *to honor the self*

MANTRAS

"I trust the Universe, I trust the will of God"

SO HUM/HAM SA: *to connect to your breath*

YA RAHMAN O YA RAHIM: *to call to the Benevolent*

OM HANSAM HANSAHA: *for good health*

SATNAM: *to connect to your higher truth*

"I surrender to Thy will"

AAH: *to invoke confidence*

Chant the name of the Divine, in any way that you wish

MEDITATION/VISUALIZATION

(OPTIONAL: "FLAME MEDITATION" WITH THE USE OF A CANDLE)

Through slow inhalation and exhalation of your breath, allow your mind to find its quiet. Visualize a golden light around your womb and

see it being strengthened and healed as the light travels through your
entire body. Feel the warm radiance of the light, and in it, find comfort
and healing.

Note: please replace "he" and "him" with
"she" and "her" if applicable.

Oh empty womb,
I grieve for my baby.

In the past days and weeks,
I felt his spirit,
but now he is gone.
I feel the emptiness within me.

I dreamt so much for us,
but today,
I feel lost without him.

I cannot understand why this happened,
and I pray
that I will find my peace.

Oh little one,
I wanted to love you
and show you so much.
I wanted to be your mother,
your guide,
your friend.
I did not get the chance to see you.
It was not meant to be.

Forever
you will remain in my heart.

Till we meet again,
my child,
be in joy and at peace,
as you rest in the arms of God.
I was blessed to know you,
even if our time together was short.

Dear God,
my heart is saddened,
as the blood flows through my body
for its final release.
Help me surrender my pain
to the skies, dust, and winds.

I trust that I will heal from this,
as you cradle me in love.
I know I am protected by You.
I know I am guided.

I honor the hand of time
and know
that with its passage,
I will slowly begin to feel whole
once again.

Oh God,
help me see the light within me.

May faith be my anchor
always.

This is my prayer
as I sit at Your gate,
embracing the wisdom
of Your ways.

Always,
in You
I trust.

Amen

COPING WITH THE SUDDEN LOSS
OF A LOVED ONE

The experience of losing someone suddenly to an unexpected incident—such as a crime, suicide, accident, or natural disaster—is beyond what we can ever imagine. The shock and grief from such a tragedy can be excruciatingly difficult to process and accept. During such times, support becomes critical; we must turn to family, friends, and others in our communities and seek the help of a bereavement counselor, spiritual teacher, and/or support group to help us heal and find our way back to life.

Praying and creating sacred space each day can help us find peace and serve as a reminder that physical death does not signify the end of life but rather its continuation in a different form. Remember that we

never lose those we love: we carry them in our hearts. Their love will
always reside within us, and one day we will be reunited with them.

Note: please replace "he" and "him" with
"she" and "her" if applicable.

STONES TO USE

HEMATITE/ARAGONITE: *to lend support in moments of high*
anxiety or hysteria

MALACHITE/ONYX/TOPAZ/TOURMALINE: *to strengthen,*
to ground

JADE: *to support feelings of security*

MOSS AGATE: *to soothe, to lift the spirits*

SNOW QUARTZ: *to bring forth calm*

ZOISITE: *to aid in relieving lethargy*

GARNET/RUBY: *to relieve depression, to revitalize after initial*
stages of grief

MANTRAS

"Spirit lives on, love never dies"
Chant the name of the Divine, in any way that you wish

MEDITATION/VISUALIZATION
(OPTIONAL: "FLAME MEDITATION" WITH THE USE OF A CANDLE)

In time, visualize your loved one with light around him. Embrace
him and tell him that you love him. Let this feeling anchor and calm
you, knowing your loved one is always with you.

Dear God,
I come to Your house

in utter disbelief,
frozen and speechless,
shattered . . .
broken to pieces.
My loved one is gone.

I never envisioned such a tragedy.
I cannot understand or accept it.
I know not how to make sense of it,
cope with it, live with it . . .
this unfathomable loss,
this immense pain.

Oh Spirit,
I cannot think clearly.
My mind seems incapable.
My entire being suddenly feels aged . . .
unable to talk,
unable to walk,
unable to live with this pain.

I turn to You, oh Lord,
for there is no other but You.
Please receive my prayer.
Please help me.
Please grant me peace,
even if for a moment in time.

Anchor me in my faith,
so I may understand
that this life is not final,

but a continuation . . .
and that one day,
I will unite with my loved one,
once again.

Oh Beloved,
I pray he is at peace,
nestled in Your embrace,
immersed in a love that is
beyond my imagination . . .

Please let him know
that I love him,
that I will carry him forever,
that I will remember and honor him,
as he would want to be.

Guide me
so I may understand
that he is with me
always.

I will come to You, oh Lord,
in each day,
in each hour,
calling Your name,
to find refuge in prayer,
and slowly . . .
I will grieve.
I will breathe again.
I will find acceptance

through Your grace,
through the hands of time . . .

Dear God,
I lay upon the gates of Your love.
Please receive my heart's prayer.
Please deliver me this peace.

With this,
I sit.

Shokran . . . Amen

FOR THE LOSS OF A COMPANION ANIMAL

The bond between a human being and a companion animal can be very powerful, as it is rooted in an unconditional love—one that touches the deepest and purest place within us. The passing of such a beloved friend can be devastatingly difficult. During such times, we need to honor our grief and allow time to heal our broken hearts. The life we shared with a companion animal will always remain a blessing, despite his or her physical absence.

STONES TO USE

HEMATITE/ARAGONITE: *to relieve severe anxiety and stress*
JADE: *to support feelings of security*
AMBER: *to soothe and lift your spirit*

MALACHITE/JASPER/ONYX/TOPAZ: *to strengthen your spirit, to contain your emotions*

TOURMALINE: *to understand our placement in the sphere of the Universe*

GIRASOL: *to bring forth inner joy after grieving*

SNOW QUARTZ: *to calm, to restore balance*

RUBY/GARNET: *to ease depression, to rejuvenate*

MANTRAS

"Love lives on, spirit lives on"

OM: *to find peace*

Chant the name of the Divine, in any way that you wish

MEDITATION/VISUALIZATION

(OPTIONAL: "FLAME MEDITATION" WITH THE USE OF A CANDLE)

As you find your calm, imagine your companion animal. See him/ her in white light. Embrace him and speak to him about your feelings. Through this find comfort and healing.

Note: please replace "he" and "him" with "she" and "her" if applicable.

Dear Spirit,
my heart is heavy as I come to You,
for I have lost my best friend,
my confidant,
my joy.

I am lost without him.
I loved him so purely and fully.
I miss him so deeply,

each minute,
each day.

I feel an emptiness,
a deep loss.
I cannot imagine
how the day will break
without him.

I see his beaming face,
his meaningful gaze,

in each corner of the room.
I long to hold him in my arms
once again.

Dear God,
bless him
as He crosses over
to join You.
As he finds peace and joy
in Your embrace,
may he know
how deeply I loved him . . .
and always will.

Thank You, dear God,
for him,
and for the precious gift of his friendship
that You bestowed upon me.

His unconditional love,
his being,
will always be part of me.

I learned so much from him
and grew so much with him.
I am wiser,
richer, and better
for knowing him.
He opened my heart in ways
that no other could.

I pray that I will feel his presence
in the days, months, and years ahead.
I pray that he will visit me in my sleep.

I know that one day,
I will embrace him again,
but for today and the days ahead,
dear Spirit,
I ask You to grant me strength and courage.

Help me release this pain.
Help me accept that this is the cycle of life,
and that it was his time to go.
Help me see and hold on
to the joyous memories
I shared with him.

I know he is smiling down on me.
He was my angel here, on Earth,
and now,
he is my guiding angel
from the Heavens.

I love you,
my precious one . . .
and always will.

Namaste

power of togetherness
and prayer

A dear colleague and friend—a spiritual teacher and pillar in the community—was facing the challenge of her life: her daughter had been diagnosed with cancer. At first, the news came like a bolt of lightning, but there was much hope that the illness might be healed. Also, the daughter was herself a "light-worker"—a young woman spiritually evolved beyond her years, revered by all who knew her. Surely, *she* would heal.

This mother plunged deep into all kinds of activities to assist her daughter's cause. She organized a number of community gatherings for prayer, meditation, and emotional support, as well as fund-raisers to help with the escalating medical expenses. The community responded and came together, each time creating a synergy of healing for this remarkable young woman. Communal chants, prayers, and song strengthened our resolve, and thus, as a strong pillar, we stood unwavering, unshakeable. We remained hopeful with each passing month.

During a period of two years, the young woman slowly walked into her spiritual healing. She heard the whispers of her soul calling her to truly become whole. As she came to terms with her illness, she shed her emotional barriers one by one. She started healing the relationships in her life; what before had been ignored no longer could be, as the realization that there may not be much time left became more apparent each day.

As the seasons turned and the second year arrived, the chance for a "cure" seemed dimmer and dimmer. Yet the community events continued, and each of us rallied support from our e-mail lists and prayer sites, as we held her continually in the healing white light of our minds and hearts.

As we gathered, praying, meditating, and chanting for her, a portal within each of us opened up, and we all began noticing huge shifts within ourselves. The healing power of the prayers was palpable, and each time we prayed for her healing, we could feel our own healing take place.

At one particular event, where spiritual leaders had gathered for communal chants and prayer, we were so inspired by her growth and elevation that it felt like she had become the teacher and we the students. In a very interesting way, we had been reawakened through her illness. As our chain became stronger, our voices no longer needed to be loud, for our silence held our soul's prayers. And as we became more centered for her, we became more centered in Light; each day we learned from her grace, her forgiveness, and her wisdom.

Even as she drew her last breath in this life, we were all in prayer for her being. At her memorial service, the late-afternoon sky was a blue veil of divine light, as a sacred quality of joy and peace danced in the air. Her presence was all around us, in the rustling of leaves and the ocean breeze. And when they released balloons, the sky seemed to open up . . . and we could feel her smiling down upon us.

For many months after her transition, those who had seen or

known her spoke of her angelic quality. Her passing had, in a way, opened channels of deeper understanding of the unknowns in life and led each of us into a dance with Spirit. We had come together as a community to give the gift of healing to a dear sister, and through this sacred process, we received the gift of healing ourselves.

After all, we are all links of the same chain.

prayers
for special
occasions

FOR A FUNERAL

Losing a loved one can be extremely difficult, and the grieving process may take much time. However, funerals can provide some healing and help us understand, on a deeper level, that our loved ones have moved on to the next chapter and are at peace. Allow yourself this sacred time.

STONES TO USE

ONYX/MALACHITE/TOPAZ: *to give strength at the most trying moments*

ROSE QUARTZ/SNOW QUARTZ: *to calm and create inner balance*

HEMATITE/ARAGONITE: *to ease extreme anxiety*

MANTRAS

SO HUM/HAM SA: *to connect to the breath of being*

YA HAYY O YA HAQQ: *to understand and accept the cycle of life and afterlife*

OM: *for peace*

"We live on in God's embrace"

"Peace be with me, peace be with you, peace be with us"

WAKAN TANKA: *to connect to the Unseen*

Chant the name of the Divine, in any way that you wish

MEDITATION/VISUALIZATION

Imagine your loved one surrounded by light. Embrace him/her and feel the love calm your being.

Note: please replace "he" and "him" with "she" and "her" if applicable.

Oh Light Divine,
Please receive our prayer for [name of deceased].

We all come forth from You,
and return to Your loving arms.
We come with this knowledge,
and return to You richer,
elevated in spirit,
more enlightened by our experience here, on Earth.

Oh God,
today, as we come to You, our dear [name of deceased]
has journeyed from this earthly plane
to Your Heavenly Realm.

May he be at peace,
knowing he was loved and honored.

May he be in joy,
as he is greeted by loved ones on the other side,
held in their warm embrace.

Beloved,
bless him as he joins You
in Your ultimate grace.

May Your angels carry him
on their wings,
to the only true home:
Your divine embrace.

May his spirit be in peace,
as he rests in Your Heavenly Skies.
And as he awakens,
may he find a joy in being home,
nestled in Your love.

Dear God,
please receive our prayer,
as You receive Your child.

Shokran . . . Amen

FOR THE ANNIVERSARY OF THE PASSING OF A LOVED ONE

By honoring and remembering our loved ones on the anniversary of their passing, we can feel their presence more profoundly and connect more deeply to their spirit and to the love we shared with them. Taking a few moments in our daily lives to acknowledge such days can bring healing and comfort to us, and bring joy to our loved ones in the spirit world.

My dear [name of the deceased],
today
is the anniversary
of the day you joined God
in the realm of the Divine.

Today,
I sit in remembrance of you,

with your face,
your name,
upon my heart.

I pray that your soul is at peace,
your spirit joyous,
in the arms of the Beloved.

Forever,
I shall honor you,
love you,
and miss you . . .
your voice and laughter,
your beautiful face,
your eyes full of stories,
your presence.

Our love and caring are my strength and anchor
on trying days,
and the smile upon my lips
on days of ease.
The memories
we share are my forever treasure.
I cherish you . . .
always.

When I close my eyes,
I can see you . . .
your magical being
dancing into my heart.
I know you are smiling

from the Heavens.
You are my guardian angel.
This,
I know.

My beautiful one,
I love you and I embrace you . . .
always.

Namaste

FOR A GRADUATION

Graduating from high school or college is a very important event in life. During this time of transition, young people can benefit greatly from receiving guidance, support, and prayers. The gift of prayer may open up a lifetime of faith, anchoring young lives and establishing hope and love in their hearts.

My dear [insert name or relation],
I have awaited this day for many years.
I have dreamt of it,
hoped for it,
and finally,
today
it is here:
a celebration of you.

I am proud of you,
for your hard work,
for the person you have become,
for this accomplishment.
And now, before you lies an endless field . . .
full of promise,
full of hope.

I pray that today
and each day going forward,
you find meaning in your steps,
hear the whisper of your soul,
and live your life in its highest truth.

I pray that you always see the light within,
know that you are special
in the eyes of God.

I pray that faith be your anchor
and guide you
through the hills and valleys you cannot see.

I pray that you walk through life with clarity,
and that when confused,
you pause to find the quiet space within,
connecting to your core
and to the Universe.

I pray that on stormy days,
you replace fear with love,
despair with hope.

May you always open your heart to Love,
to kindness,
to compassion,
to life.

May you touch many with your heart
and know that your life can make a difference
to those around you
and to the world.

May you continue to grow, to learn, to elevate
and be full of wonder . . .
always seeing the blessings of life
in each corner, in each turn.

I love you,
and I pray that you will know,
always,
that God is with you.
He will walk with you,
lift you,
and guide you
every step of the way . . .
always.

FOR A WEDDING

Love is always a divine gift, and to honor it as such is holy. Embrace and honor your wedding day by creating a sacred space of prayer before your ceremony, basking together in the joy of your union.

Spirit,
You have bestowed upon us
a most precious of blessings . . .
the gift of love.

You have led us to one another
and awakened us
to the whisper of our hearts . . .
to a joy we knew not before . . .
to a love that has anchored us,
strengthened us,
inspired us to new heights of being.

Today,
we will stand
united,
hand in hand,
to make a promise,
as we take the sacred vows of marriage.

Grace us, oh God,
with Your blessing . . .
May our union be guided
by Your light.
May we remain always
in this holy space of togetherness.

May our bond deepen,
as we revel in songs of joy
and face the tides of change,

with unwavering commitment
to one another.

May we grow together
yet honor the spaces between us,
while journeying hand in hand,
respecting our individuals paths
and the truth that resides
within each of our hearts.

May we trust one another
with our dreams and wishes,
our thoughts and feelings,
our fears and trepidations.

May we be the strength
for one another—
be pillars to lean on . . .
pillars of faith,
of truth,
standing tall,
upholding the sanctuary
of our marriage.

May we be in good health,
and bask in the glorious peace
of our union,
our life together,
each day.

May we be understanding and patient,
kind and giving,
honoring our vows of love.

May we never lose sight of You,
and may this blessing be upon us,
today and always.

Spirit,
we stand together
in Your light,
and in gratitude,
we humbly bow
to Your infinite grace.

Amen

FOR A WEDDING ANNIVERSARY

Dear God,
on this day,
[the number of] year(s) ago,
we rejoiced in our union,
coming together,
hand in hand,
in holy matrimony,
promising one another
our hearts and our lives.

Today,
as we celebrate
and honor the anniversary
of our wedding,
we bow to You,
thankful and humbled,
with joy and gratitude
upon our hearts.

God, we do not take Your blessing for granted.

You have guided us each day
on this journey,
through hills and valleys,
through dark nights
and days full of hope and promise.

You have led us always,
into the place of light,
so we forget not the love that resides
at the core of our union.

And today,
we pray . . .

Dear Spirit,
may our home be a sanctuary
and our hearts be a temple
of the gift of love
You have bestowed upon us.

May we honor
the spaces and differences
between us,
and the togetherness
we share.

May our understanding
of one another grow,
our love deepen,
our bond strengthen,
through the hand of time.

As we build more memories,
may we cherish and enjoy the journey,
embracing it with each step.

May we see joy
in the smallest of moments
and remember
that each day of our togetherness
is a blessing from You.
And our love . . .
is our forever treasure.

As we sit
with Your grace,
oh Divine,
we bow
in gratitude.

Amen

BLESSINGS FOR A NEW HOME

Our home is our haven—a sanctuary where our spirit and body can rest, replenish, and rejuvenate. Start your life in a new home with prayers and blessings to help create a greater sense of grounding and joy.

STONES TO USE

JADE: *to foster feelings of security (place in small bowls in the more significant rooms of your home)*

ROSE QUARTZ: *to support love and kindness (place in bedrooms and other significant rooms)*

Oh Mother Divine:
Bless this home with Your grace.
Bless this home with Your love.
Bless this home
as a sanctuary,
a temple of peace,
where we can rest our souls
and come to You,
always.

May this home ring with laughter and good health.
May this home ring with sounds of joy and peace.
May this home be a haven of faith and truth.
May this home be lit always,
with Your light.

Bless this home, oh Spirit,
and all who cross its threshold.

Protect and shield us from outside harm.
Bless us with inner peace and newfound hope.

As we make this house our home,
we shall reside in it,
with Your light.

Bless this home,
Mother Divine,
with Your grace and love,
always.

Amen

FOR ONE WHO IS PREGNANT

*Pregnancy is a sacred time in a woman's life. Honor this and allow
yourself to embrace this special journey.*

MANTRAS
 "I am of Love"
 "I carry love"
 "I behold Your miracle"
 SHALOM/OM: *for peace*

ALLAH O AKBAR: *to call to the Divine*
Chant the name of the Divine, in any way that you wish

MEDITATION/VISUALIZATION
Find your center through your breath and allow yourself to relax. Visualize light around and within your body. Envision your child healthy and happy. Feel the joy. Embrace this and sit in gratitude as you honor this journey.

Note: please replace "she" and "her" with "he" and "him" if applicable.

Goddess,
I come to You
with joy and gratitude,
for I am with child.
I sit in awe of this miracle,
this gift You have bestowed upon me.

Blessed am I
to be her vessel,
to carry her in my womb . . .
and blessed I will be
to birth her into the splendor
of our world,
and to nurture her with love.

Protect her from harm and illness
oh Beloved,
and grant her good health

of body, mind, and spirit.
May she grow with grace
and know peace,
as she blossoms within my body.
Grant me fortitude,
so I may carry her in health
and fuel her with all I have,
in every moment.

I await her beaming face,
and sit in anticipation of her birth . . .
May she come in joy,
through Light,

and with faith,
always.

I will rejoice in this miracle
of her life
I shall cradle her
and hold her upon my chest,
kissing her gently,
softly whispering words of love.
I shall sing to her
and caress her,
with the tender touch of a mother's heart.

Guide me, oh Goddess,
to teach her kindness,
truth, and compassion,
to walk her to a path
of faith and peace,
and to lead her to Your loving ways . . .
always.

This is the prayer
upon my heart . . .
Beloved,
receive us,
in Your grace.

BLESSINGS FOR THE BIRTH OF A CHILD

Note: please replace "she" and "her" with
"he" and "him" if applicable.

Dear God,
we come to You today
to welcome this beautiful, precious child,
[name of child],
who has entered our world.

Bless this angel with Your love,
oh Spirit,
as she begins her new life . . .

Bless her with good health,
of mind, body, and spirit,
and with joy of being.

Bless her with good judgment,
kindness, compassion,
and purity of heart.

Bless her with the gift
of family and friends
by her side.

I pray . . .

I pray that her heart may know
deep fulfillment and purpose,
true love and happiness.

I pray that her life may touch others,
and that she may be of service
to the world.

I pray that she may rise
above the challenges that come her way,
finding strength in her convictions
and never losing faith.

I pray that she may live in gratitude
each day,
through each breath . . .
with the knowledge
of this gift of life
and of all her blessings.

Spirit,
may Your grace
be upon her
as she grows and blossoms,
and may she live in her truth.

May her spirit know peace
and be connected to You
always.
May she grow
in her knowledge of You,
remaining in Your light.

As we welcome her
into our lives

and into our hearts, dear God,
we bow to You
in prayer.

Amen

～

FOR THE ADOPTION OF A CHILD

*The road to adoption is often one of many twists and turns, and one
that requires patience, determination, and faith. Trust in God's will,
as you navigate the path that will lead to finding your heart's child.*

STONES TO USE

AQUAMARINE: *to release anxieties and blockages*

JADE: *to foster feelings of security*

CARNELIAN: *to calm and support positive action*

MOOKAITE: *to guide your way*

ROSE QUARTZ: *to open channels of love*

LAPIS LAZULI: *to see with wisdom*

SODALITE: *to support clarity*

RUBY/GARNET: *to revitalize*

MALACHITE/ONYX: *to strengthen*

TIGER'S EYE: *to support courage and action*

MANTRAS

"I trust the divine design"

"I surrender to Thy Will"

AMMA, OMMA, OR MAA: *to connect to the Mother Divine*

ABBA/BAA: *to connect to the Father Divine*
Mangala Charan Mantra (see appendix A)

Note: please replace "she" and "her" with
"he" and "him" if applicable.

Dear God,
my soul yearns to have a child . . .
to hold her against my chest,
to caress her being
with a parent's gentle touch.

I have walked this journey,
through hours of doubt and dismay,
and found myself
at Your door.

Receive my prayer, oh Spirit . . .
lead me,
guide me,
help me,
so I may see with clarity,
so I may find the child
You have intended for me.

This child will not be of my body,
but of my heart.
Her eyes may look different from mine,
her skin may be as dark as the rich soil
or as light as daybreak,

but her heart will beat as mine,
with love.

Oh, child of my heart,
child of my destiny,
of my life . . .
hold on,
I am on my way . . .
Each day
I am closer to you.

Wait, oh little angel,
the time will come . . .
my arms will soon embrace you.

Be patient, have faith, trust . . .

Fate will deliver this to us,
as intended.
Our hearts will touch
and our souls will whisper:
We have found one another.
We are home.

I will not despair or allow defeat.
I will be patient . . .
and surrender
to the whisper of the winds,
as it guides me through the haze.

Soon we will bask in this joy,
this gift
from the heavens.
I know Spirit will guide us . . .

I trust this.
I trust the Universe.
I trust . . .
the will of God.

Namaste

TO HONOR A BIRTHDAY

Grant yourself a few minutes to honor the anniversary of the day you were born, in the quiet of your soul. Sit in gratitude for the gift of life you have been given. Reconnect to your higher purpose, gaining a fresh perspective as you step into a new year. Blessed be your day, and may you rejoice in peace and joy.

STONES TO USE
CARNELIAN/ROSE QUARTZ: *to honor the self*

MANTRAS
SO HUM/HAM SA: *to connect to the breath of life*
SATNAM: *to connect to your higher self*

MEDITATION
Breathe in and out, focusing on the gift of your breath. Enjoy and embrace the vastness of being, honoring your day and life.

Dear God,
today is the anniversary of my birth . . .
the day my earthly mother
delivered me into this physical world,
so full of wonder and colors.

I come humbly to Your door,
scattering flowers of gratitude,
with my heart so full of love.
You created me from Your light,
giving me the gift of life.
You are my Eternal Father,
my Eternal Mother.

From You,
I have come forth.
From You,
I breathe.
From You,
I am.

The years have not always been easy,
the road has not always been clear,
my heart has not always been happy,
and I have not always heard the whisper of my soul.

And yet
always . . .
You have protected me,
guided me,
loved me,

and lifted me,
when I could not.

Dear God,
I know You have chosen me to come here
for divine lessons.
Today,
as I honor and celebrate
this gift of life,
I ask that You please guide me
so I may see clearly
and find my path,
so I may always live my higher truth
and hear the magical songs of my soul.

I am full of hope,
of love,
of peace,
for I have You.

Eternally humbled
and grateful for Your grace,
on this day and every day,
I bow to You
for all You have bestowed upon me
as I chant Your name.

Amen

the awakening:
a wedding story

I was asked to ordain a wedding ceremony for a couple in their midthirties. During our initial meeting, weeks before the ceremony, the groom insisted that I not use words referring to Divinity, such as "God," "Light," or "the Beloved." He said he wanted the wedding ceremony to simply be about the institution of marriage, without the usual spiritual and religious language. His fiancée appeared to have no opinion on this matter.

I was taken aback by the groom's request, since I see marriage as a devoutly spiritual union. Still, I decided to keep things light and harmonious, in hopes of creating the appropriate space for him to change his mind on his own. So I complied but also asked him and his fiancée to consider integrating a few passages by Rumi or Khalil Gibran into the ceremony and possibly honoring some family members who had crossed over. The couple listened but did not seem interested in either of these ideas.

When I discussed this matter with the groom's parents, a few days later, they were devastated to hear about their son's decision to omit spiritual references from the ceremony—especially his father, who was an ordained minister scheduled to co-officiate the wedding with me.

"Mitra!" the father said, shocked over the news. "This cannot be! There is no way we can conduct this service without mentioning God. I won't have it!"

I understood the father's distress, but I calmly reminded him that it was his son's wedding, and we needed to honor his wishes. I also expressed to him that if his son was going to have a change of heart, it would only happen if we allowed him to reach a conclusion on his own. Resisting his decision would only cause him to be more defiant about it. His father reluctantly agreed, and we both decided to allow things to unfold naturally.

A couple of weeks later, the groom called to say he liked my suggestion of using passages from Rumi and had decided he wanted excerpts to be included. Of course, Rumi is all about love for the Divine, but I didn't feel a need to disclose specifics! Instead, I simply agreed to his request, knowing that if we continued to allow him a little space for reflection, he would very likely come around in his own time.

A week before the wedding, he called and said he also liked my suggestion about mentioning those who had crossed over, as a way of honoring them. He said he felt this was important and would like it included in the ceremony as well.

I could feel the tides shifting.

Sure enough, a couple of days before the wedding, as I was reviewing the ceremony with the bride and groom, he said that he wanted to give me free rein, and that if I wanted to use the word "God" or "Beloved," that was fine with him. I casually said okay, careful not to react too enthusiastically.

The wedding day arrived. I hadn't been in touch with his father for several days, so when I saw him that afternoon, there was real turmoil in his eyes. He still thought we had to forgo any mention of the Divine.

"Your son has come around," I told him, a grin breaking across my face. "He has given us free rein to speak of God in any way we see fit for the service!"

Immediately all the tension drained from the father's face, and he smiled wide. "Yes!" he shouted, raising his hands over his head, before giving me a big hug.

Prior to the service, the groom seemed excited, emotional, and nervous, which was very different from how I had seen him before. As is my custom, I did a special meditation with him and his bride before the ceremony. He was clasping my hand and, as we centered ourselves in a state of peacefulness and light, tears filled his eyes. I could see his soul had been awakened to something he had not allowed before. It was a magical moment.

During the ceremony, I read poems by Rumi in both Farsi and English, and used the words "God" and "Beloved," creating a sacred space for the holy covenant of marriage. As soon as I mentioned God, tears welled up in the groom's eyes, and by the second or third mention tears were streaming down his cheeks. His face lit up, and his eyes seemed to reflect a profound knowing deep within his soul—he had reconnected with God; he had unlocked the closed doorways of his heart. Now he was basking in the Light.

After the ceremony, he took me aside and said, "I am so happy you did the ceremony the way you did. I could not believe how emotional I got. It was like the whole room was lit up with light! It was beautiful!"

I thought it was beautiful as well, but not because of my words. It was beautiful because he had allowed the higher truth inside himself to be awakened. Miraculous . . .

seasonal prayers

FOR SPRING, REBIRTH, AND RENEWAL

It is time . . .

Time to awaken from a long winter night's sleep,
to open the shades and let the sun pour in,
to smell the fresh fragrance of blossoming flowers.

Time to welcome the spring showers
and dance with the rains,
to renew our promises to the earth,
and to plant new seeds of hope.

It is time . . .

Time to be in gratitude,
to recognize our blessings,
to revive our spirit.

Time to be present,
to be kind,
to refresh our soul with newfound joy.

It is time . . .

Time to walk toward our dreams,
to unite hand in hand,
to come together peacefully as one,
to celebrate life,
to dance with the winds of change.

Dear Mother Divine,
may our spirits soar to new heights,
may we fly to new plateaus of awareness,
may our lives be joyous
and our actions reflect love,
and may we walk,
always,
with a peaceful strength.

Now is the time . . .

In these first days of spring,
may we honor our promises to ourselves,
turn our heads to the skies in prayer,
and open our arms to the magical possibilities
of this season,
of renewal,
of life.

This
is our prayer,
whispered to the wind.

FOR THE FALL EQUINOX

*On the eve of the fall equinox, let us welcome the birth of a new season
into our lives with clarity, purity, and sacred thought by centering ourselves through meditation and prayer. Autumn is a time of harvest, a
time to reflect, to release, and to put our lives in order.*

MANTRAS

"I surrender to Thy will"

"I give my fears to the winds to carry"

"I give my doubts to the river to wash away"

SO HUM/HAM SA: *to connect to the breath of life and the
    Universe*

SATNAM: *to connect to your higher truth*

OM: *for peace*

Chant the name of the Divine, in any way that you wish

MEDITATION/VISUALIZATION

(OPTIONAL: "FLAME MEDITATION" WITH THE USE OF A CANDLE)

(RECOMMENDED ADDITION: "WALKING MEDITATION")

*Find your calm through your breath. Envision that which no longer
serves you. Imagine giving it to the winds to carry away and giving it
to the river to wash away. Feel the liberation of this. Embrace it.*

Dear Light of Lights,
on this magical eve
we turn to You,
welcoming and embracing
this season of harvest.

As leaves change color
and the cool breeze sets in,
please guide us to release
the fears and trepidations
we are holding on to,
and replace them
with courage and purpose.

Help us harvest
and share the abundance
of past seasons with all,
with generosity of spirit.

Dear God,
we step into this night
with much gratitude,
with knowledge and wisdom gained,
and with the hope
that we may bring forth
a more meaningful,
peaceful existence
in the months ahead.

As we begin this new season,
guide us,
oh Spirit.

May we walk into
a more fulfilled life,
one that is great
in its simple moments,
blessed with the knowledge that
today is a gift . . .
to be lived in grace,
with family and friends,
and all who we encounter
in our lives.

May we see the dawn of hope,
even in the darkest of nights,
and may we be the light bearers,
carrying Your love to all,
in each step,
in each turn.

May we live our lives
in the truth of who we are,
in the joy of being,
and in gratitude
for Your endless blessings.

We thank You
for this moment . . .
for all we have,
for all there is,
and for all that may be . . .

With this,
we sit,
on this autumn eve,
humbly,
in prayer.

Amen

FOR HOLY DAYS

Holy days in various cultures around the world are sacred times for the soul and often serve as opportunities for self-reflection—moments to be present with our higher selves and to connect with the Divine.

Beloved,
we come to You today,
in remembrance of this holy occasion,
with prayer in our hearts,
honoring this sacred time.

Guide us,
so we may recall the history
and the lessons learned and shared,
so we may reflect
on the deepest meaning
of this day.

May Your blessings
of joy and love
always be upon each of us,
and may we live
a life of truth and goodness,
in joy and health,
anchored in self-realization
and faith.

With this,
we sit in prayer,
honoring this holy day.

FOR THE NEW YEAR

It is upon us: the birth of a new year, the awakening of our hopes, dreams, and aspirations.

As we come close to the final days of the year, let us reflect on the experiences we have had, with their challenges and many blessings. Let us remember all those who walked into our lives and hearts: those who are here and those who are no longer with us, but are in the realm of spirit, guiding our way. Let us remember the grace we were shown each day, always lifted by the arms of many, and always lifted by God. Let us carry this love and gratitude into the new year. We have grown, we have gained wisdom, and now we can apply this to what lies ahead. Let us offer our hearts in prayer as we begin anew.

MANTRAS
"We are children of the Light"
"We are of Light"
OM HANSAM HANSAHA: *for protection of health*
Gayatri Mantra (see appendix A)
SO HUM/HAM SA: *to connect to the breath of life*
OM: *for peace*
Chant the name of the Divine, in any way that you wish

MEDITATION/VISUALIZATION
(OPTIONAL: "FLAME MEDITATION" WITH THE USE OF A CANDLE)
Breathe in and out, and find your calm. Visualize a white light within and all around you. Extend this to your neighborhood, city, country, and the world. Inhale and exhale peace and healing.

Dear God,
as we walk into this new year,
we pray that we never lose sight
of Your grace,
and that Your light
be revealed to us
always.

We pray
that You bless us all
with harmony, joy,
and good health.

We pray
that we live
in the truth of who we are,
and that our path be protected and lit
in our journey each day.

We pray
that we find the courage
to follow our dreams
and our souls' calling,
and that faith and patience
anchor us,
in times of turbulence.

We pray
that ill feelings and thoughts
be removed from our hearts,

and be replaced
by forgiveness and love.

Oh Divine,
we pray
that we never become so self-involved
that we walk away
from another's pain.

We pray
that the peace and joy we feel
transcend this moment,
and become the calm
that will be upon
all nations and people.

May the grace that is
bestowed upon each of us,
the love that resides
within each soul,
and the selflessness and kindness
revealed by sages, prophets,
and messengers of peace,
be the light
in our journey
each day.

Oh dear Spirit,
may each inhale and exhale of breath
be of gratitude . . .
may Your truth

lead our way . . .
and may our hope give birth
to new dreams . . .

May peace be upon the earth,
joy be upon the world,
and love be upon our hearts
as we embark upon a new year,
with Your grace.

Amen

FOR THE NEW MOON

The new moon occurs two weeks before the full moon but, initially, cannot be seen by the naked eye. In some cultures, this period is considered a favorable time for new beginnings. Use the new moon period to connect with your higher self, identifying your innermost dreams and desires, and taking steps to move forward in manifesting them.

STONES TO USE

AMETHYST/FLUORITE: *to open the channels within*

TURQUOISE: *to connect to the higher self*

LAPIS LAZULI: *to open to new visions, to connect to higher wisdom*

TIGER'S EYE: *to support positive action*

MANTRAS

SO HUM/HAM SA: *to connect to the breath of your being*

SATNAM: *to connect to your higher self*

OM: *to open yourself to meditation and the vastness of thought*
   and being
Chant the name of the Divine, in any way that you wish

MEDITATION/VISUALIZATION
(OPTIONAL: "FLAME MEDITATION" WITH THE USE OF A CANDLE)
   As you inhale and exhale, find your calm. Allow your mind and
heart to focus on your dreams and wishes. Embrace them and envision
taking steps in your daily life toward manifesting them.

Oh Moon,
as you are hiding tonight,
beneath the thin veil of the skies,
biding your time,
I sit,
in anticipation
of your radiant beauty.

Soon you will reveal
your silvery silhouette,
once again
mesmerizing all
and enchanting the world.

Oh goddess of the skies,
on this magical night,
I sit with you in quiet,
gathering my thoughts
and reflecting on all that I desire.

With your rebirth,
I wish to reawaken old promises
and bring forth new dreams.
I wish to plant new seeds
in the garden of my life,
and watch them bloom
into a bed of magical colors.

As I walk toward your new cycle,
I honor my spirit and body,

embracing the gift of breath
and the covenant of Truth.

I pray to live a richer life . . .
one of love, laughter, and faith,
one of wisdom, service, compassion,
and good health.

I pray for my soul to know
its calling,
its yearning,
its truth,
always,
as I connect deeper
with Spirit.

Oh Enchantress of the Skies,
I surrender to you,
as I walk toward a life
blessed with grace,
with newfound hope in my heart.

I sit with you,
embracing this beauty all around me . . .
honoring the silent quiet of my mind,
the joy of my heart,
and the breath of creation itself.

Patiently
I await

the bewitching splendor . . .
that is you.

⌣

FOR THE FULL MOON

The full moon is a magical time each month. In some cultures, it is celebrated as a period of reflection and release, and of bringing forth our wishes and dreams. During the full moon period release your stress and anxieties, and allow your spirit to be refreshed and renewed through devotion.

MANTRAS
"I surrender to Thy splendor"
"To Thy will I surrender"
SO HUM / HAM SA: *to connect to the breath of being*
OM: *to align with the Universe*
WAKAN TANKA: *to connect to all there is*

MEDITATION/VISUALIZATION
(OPTIONAL: "FLAME MEDITATION" WITH THE USE OF A CANDLE)
(RECOMMENDED ADDITION: "WALKING MEDITATION")
Inhale and exhale gently. Slowly, take deeper breaths and release all pent-up energies. Sit in the vastness of being, in the quiet of stillness. Embrace this. Open your heart to reflection and devotion.

Dear Goddess of the Skies,
today,
as I sit in your glory,
in the completion of your cycle,

I am mystified
by your radiant beauty.

Your full silver body
nestles in the sky
and mesmerizes the world.
I sit in awe of you,
in reflection . . .
in thought . . .
in prayer.

Oh Enchanting Moon,
I turn to you tonight,
yearning to clear
all patterns of thought
that no longer serve me.

As I chant Spirit's name,
I wish to release all my fears
and remove all blockages on my path,
so I may see with more clarity.

Tonight,
I release my anxiety,
shedding the layers of pain,
accepting and allowing transformation,
and embracing a new vision.

To the winds of the night,
I give my fears and doubts,
releasing negative patterns of thought,

and ask that they be carried away
to the distant shores of yesterdays . . .

And with this,
I shall bring forth faith,
I shall bring forth promise,
I shall bring forth hope,
for a more enlightened life,
living each day with grace.

I pray . . .
to always be guided by Light,
to spend my days and nights
connecting with my higher self.

And I pray
that as your crescent grows
to fullness once again,
I come closer to embracing
and realizing
my deepest hopes and wishes.

Oh Goddess of the Skies,
guide me to serve,
to be part of the healing of this earth.

I pray for this,
as I pray for all . . .
for our unity,

our good health,
and our peace.

In joy,
I sit,
with your bewitching silhouette,
as you dance magically,
illuminating the skies,
mesmerizing all
who gaze upon you.

Namaste

TO CONNECT WITH DIVINE MOTHER EARTH

From Mother Earth, we draw our nourishment and well-being. Our very survival depends on her and the endless gifts she blesses us with each day. Let us sit with, honor, and connect to her sacredness.

Oh Mother,
you . . .
who gives us the gift of life
in each moment,
as we breathe in
your love . . .

You . . .
who nourishes us
and quenches our thirst . . .

You . . .
divine,
selfless,
loving . . .

You are Earth . . .
nurturer of all living beings,
mother of the soil and water,
gardener of all this richness.

Your flowers
bloom in gardens of wonder,
gifting us joy,
and your green meadows
rejuvenate our senses.

Your forests and jungles
reveal your hidden treasures
and mysteries,
and your deserts promise us
the quiet of sacred space.

Your moonlit skies
and starlit nights
beckon us to an inner awakening,
opening our hearts and minds
to new visions,
full of promise;
and your light,
each day,
births at dawn, unto the endless sky,

guiding our way,
warming our hearts.

Your clouds capture our dreams,
and lift them to the heavens,
and your winds whisper to us
of things to come.

Your snow and rains
cleanse the air we breathe
and purify the ground beneath us
with the promise of spring,
renewal,
and rebirth;
and your ocean tides
reflect our hearts' desires,
yearning always
for the Infinite.

I sit,
bowing to your ways,
as I pray . . .

I pray
for my soul
to always remain connected
to your pulse,
and for my spirit to hear
the rhythm of your seasons.

I pray
for my heart

to hear the wisdom
of the rustling leaves,
beckoning me to release
and unveil my truth.

I pray
for my mind
to embrace your endless sky . . .
its quiet,
its rumbles,
its cries,
its rejoicing rains.

And I pray
that as I journey,
my senses will be awakened
to your grace . . .
through each pebble,
each blade of grass,
each wildflower.

Oh Mother Earth,
I honor you . . .
I bow to you
in deep gratitude
for your wisdom,
your love,
your abundant heart.

I remain . . .
forever humbled.

rebel spirit, tender heart

One afternoon, I was teaching a workshop at a training center for a nonprofit organization in the Middle East. The young women filling up the room had each faced tremendous adversity and were now living together in a housing facility off-site. During the day, they came to the center to learn various life and career skills.

I was presenting a workshop on creating sacred space through prayer, meditation, and affirmations. Just before we were about to begin, a petite woman, around nineteen or twenty years of age, sluggishly entered the room, clearly not wanting to be there. Her jet-black hair was teased up over a half a foot above her head, and her face was heavily made up. Everything about her appearance and demeanor said "rebel."

She sprawled in her chair in a disrespectful manner (which is quite uncommon in this region of the world), then quickly raised her hand.

"I'm tired and don't want to listen to you. I'm going to go to sleep," she said rather impolitely, before placing her head on the desk and closing her eyes.

"That's fine; just go to sleep," I replied, consciously not

wanting to engage in her lack of respect for me or the class. I have taught for over two decades, and as a teacher and intuit I can read between the layers and words. I knew this girl lacked self-esteem and that the tough exterior was there to hide her pain.

About ten minutes into the presentation, she raised her hand—eyes semiclosed—and asked me rather defiantly if it was okay not to want to marry or have children. I told her we each have a different journey in life, and there are no specific rules that apply to every person—that God has a purpose for each of us.

A few minutes later, she raised her hand again and while maintaining her brash attitude, asked, "So you are telling me it is okay if I do not follow what other girls my age do?"

I knew she was in search of a deeper reassurance, wanting to know that there were other pathways available to her. So I said, "Yes, it's okay. You do not have to follow the norm. Each person weaves a different tapestry."

She got quiet and studied me for a moment. "I like you," she said. "You are old, like an antique, but cool!" Then she smiled, and *there* I saw a young girl—vulnerable, afraid, and unsure.

During the next part of the workshop, I could see that her tough outer layer was diminishing and she was actually interested in what I was saying. And then her hand went up for another question. "You know, I'm very confident, but when I want to do something important, like take an exam, I freeze up and feel like I cannot do well. Do you think something is wrong with me?"

"No. Many people feel anxiety before a test," I assured her.

"So you think I'm all right?" she asked.

"You are better than all right," I told her tenderly. "Look at you: you're smart, beautiful, and very witty!" Her face lit up in a smile.

"So you think I can actually do the things I want—to travel, to see the world? Am I worthy?" she asked.

"Yes," I said gently. "You are worthy. And, yes, you can do the things you dream of."

She then asked with even more vulnerability how one can really believe in herself—*know* she's worthy.

So I told her and the class more about mantras, affirmations, and meditation. She listened intently, and when the class finished, I could see she was deep in thought, pondering my words.

I went back to the center a few days later and was surprised to find this young woman running into class like a child, full of enthusiasm. "*Ostad* [master-teacher], I did it!" she yelled with a big smile. "You will be so proud of me!"

She then told me how she had created a mantra—"I am worthy"—and that silently repeating it each morning on the bus for five minutes had helped her relax throughout an exam. She also expressed to me how she had gathered some of the other young women in the house to sit and do a group meditation in the evening, and how they all felt better as a result. "It works!" she said. Then she hugged me and said thank you.

Something as simple as three words, and belief in the practice, had altered this young woman in only a few days. Now, no matter where life would take her, she had two tools—meditation and mantra—to help her, anchor her, and support her. I smile every time I think of her, and reflect, "Is this not miraculous?" All we need is to question, allow, and create to experience our own miracles.

everyday
hopes and
prayers

INVITING LOVE INTO YOUR LIFE

To open the channels to finding love and a life partner, allow your heart to remain open and embrace new possibilities. Release your fear and replace it with hope and self-love, always remembering that you are worthy. In your home, start creating physical space for another. As you cultivate this space, both internally and externally, meditate and pray daily, inviting love and partnership and surrendering to God's will.

STONES TO USE

ROSE QUARTZ: *to open the heart to love*

EMERALD: *to attract love*

CARNELIAN: *to honor the self*

MANTRAS

"I am worthy, I am worthy of love"

SATNAM: *to honor the self*

MEDITATION/VISUALIZATION

(OPTIONAL: "FLAME MEDITATION" WITH THE USE OF A CANDLE)

Inhale and exhale gently. Allow your mind to clear and open yourself to the vastness of being. Imagine a field, full of color. Feel your heart open. Feel the radiant glow of the sun pour into your heart. Envision yourself sitting in this splendor, embracing a love partner. Feel its joy and peace.

Dear God,
my heart yearns for my soul partner,
my earthly beloved,
my other half . . .

I am ready to embrace,
to nurture,
and to love wholly.

I am ready to receive
this divine gift,
to open my heart
and the gateway
of my life
to this.

I pray for a beloved
who can see me
through the eyes of the heart,
and understand my soul . . .
honoring me for who I am,
as created by Your love.

I pray that we shall walk
hand in hand,
joyously,
lovingly,
respecting and appreciating
one another,
in gratitude
of our togetherness.

I pray,
oh Spirit,
for a love that will remain
through time,

deepening and strengthening
each day.

I will cherish and treasure
such a blessing
with my entire being,
and humbly ask You,
with all I am,
to help bring this forth,
as intended by You.

This is my wish,
the prayer I lay
at Your door . . .
And with this,
I shall remain.

Amen

IN THE HOUSE OF THE BELOVED: HONORING THE SACRED SPACE OF LOVE

In this inspirational piece, the soul is yearning for a romantic love that will honor not only his/her true self, but also the sacred triangle of lovers and God. This sacred space is . . . the House of the Beloved.

My heart was not made to be
broken, bruised, or injured . . .

it is a sacred place,
only to be embraced
with love and devotion,
in the grace of Divine Light.

I honor myself.
I honor my heart.
I honor my body.
I honor my intelligence.
I honor all that I am,
all that I have worked for,
and all that I have.
I have earned this
through sweat and tears.

I am blessed . . .

Blessed to know
that my deepest truth resides only
in the House of the Beloved.
Blessed to be full of love and compassion.
Blessed to know the difference
between friend and foe,
love and temptation,
faith and fear.

If you wish to enter the House of the Beloved with me,
you must take off your shoes
and walk gently into this sacred space . . .
You must come with pure intentions and heart.
You must be here to love me,

as intended by Spirit,
and let me love you.

Here,
there is no room for fear,
for where there is love,
there is no fear,
there is no anger, pride, or ego.
For between you and me,
will only be Spirit.

This is what I wish,
what I pray for,
what I honor,
what I yearn for—
one who will treasure
and cherish
our gift of love,
through the hands of time.

No questions asked,
just love embraced.

Blessed,
we shall sit,
enveloped by the light.

Namaste

FOR ONE WHO WISHES
TO BECOME PREGNANT

Pregnancy is the miracle of life. Open your spirit and body to this sacred gift. Allow your energy to flow into a place of love, and there, surrender and trust the will of God.

STONES TO USE

AMETHYST: *to open the channels of fertility*

MOONSTONE: *to allow the goddess energy within to flow*

CARNELIAN: *to honor the self and all we create*

ROSE QUARTZ: *to open the heart to love*

MANTRAS

"I embrace Thy will"

"I embrace love"

OM: *for peace*

OM HANSAM HANSAHA: *for good health*

ONG SO HUNG: *to open the heart to the love that resides within you*

MEDITATION/VISUALIZATION

As you find your center through your breath, imagine a healing white light all within and around you. Feel your heart and body opening, and embrace the light. Visualize yourself happy, at peace, and joyous, surrendering to the rhythms of the Universe. Envision yourself pregnant. Enjoy and embrace this joy.

Note: please replace "he" and "him" with
"she" and "her" if applicable.

Oh Mother Divine,
I kneel before You,
as I have come with
a deep wish,
a sacred prayer
within my heart.
Please hear me,
and receive my prayer.

Oh Spirit,
my soul and body are longing
to receive the miracle of life.

My entire being is yearning to bear a child . . .
to carry him in my body,
to caress him with my spirit,
to give him life.

To be honored as such
is my deepest wish.

I am ready,
waiting,
each day,
to embrace his spirit,
to caress his soul
with a mother's touch.

May he grow in my womb
with Your grace,

and enter the world
in good health.
May he be blessed with a spirit
and life that will be of joy and peace.

I will love him unconditionally,
with all I am.
I will teach him Your teachings,
I will always guide him to Your light.

Oh Mother,
I wish
for him to choose me,
to come forth through me,
to rejoice with me
as he enters this world.

Please grant me this,
with ease of body
and joy of spirit.
Please deliver this blessing
upon me.

This is my prayer.
I await Your miracle . . .
I surrender to Your will.

BLESSINGS FOR A YOUNG LOVED ONE

So many wishes I have for you,
so many prayers,
so many hopes and dreams,
all wrapped in love and joy.

May the light
that shines within your heart
envelop you each day,

may you learn to love who you are,
and may you see your beauty.

May you not look back with regret,
and not look ahead with fear,
but rather swim in the sea of moments,
cherishing each experience,
living fully and richly,
embracing all.

I wish for you
to take care of the gift of life,
to share with others
your soul and heart,
to let not anxieties
cloud your mind.

I wish for your spirit to soar with hope,
in hours of darkness and dismay.

I pray that
you are always kind
to the earth,
to all creatures,
large and small.

I pray that
you learn to forgive,
not only others,
but yourself,

and to release yourself
of guilt, shame, and regret.

I hope that
you spend time laughing
with your loved ones,
and always have
a shoulder to cry on.

I hope that
you believe in yourself
and in the angels from above.

I pray that
your soul finds fulfillment,
treasuring each day and night.

I pray that you become
more aware of your calling,
of your destiny in this life,
that you grow closer to God . . .
allowing Spirit to be your guide.

I pray that you know
you can make a difference
in this world
and help others
in need.

And I pray that
you never forget to dream,

never forget to feel,
never forget that you are
a special child of God.

Soar . . .
Push the clouds aside.
You will see that
what is awaiting you
is an abundance of sunshine . . .
radiating,
glowing,
beaming . . .

This
is your life.

FOR SAFE TRAVELS

We sometimes experience anxiety or concern when a loved one is taking a trip. During such times, positive thought, meditation, and prayer can greatly support us in attaining calm and balance. This prayer can also be used for ourselves before or during travels.

STONES TO USE

JADE: *to foster feelings of security*

AQUAMARINE: *for protection when traveling around or over water*

ONYX/MALACHITE: *to contain anxiety, to create strength and balance*

SNOW QUARTZ/GIRASOL: *to calm anxieties, to bring forth optimism*

TURQUOISE: *to bring forth protection*

TOPAZ: *to keep negative thoughts away, to strengthen*

JASPER: *to protect*

ARAGONITE: *to relieve anxiety and stress*

MANTRAS

"The light is within, the light is around"

"God is always with me"

SHALOM/OM: *for peace*

OM HANSAM HANSAHA: *for health protection*

NAM MYOHO RENGE KYO: *to build confidence and strength, for several days before your travels*

MEDITATION/VISUALIZATION

Inhale and exhale to release anxiety. Do this a few times, elongating the inhale and releasing the exhale slowly with each breath. Visualize your loved ones (or yourself) traveling. Hold them (or yourself) and the vessels of transport in your mind's eye, with light within and all around. Imagine the mode of transport as a bird of love that carries your loved ones (or yourself) closer to the destination and goal.

Note: please replace "he" and "him" with "she" and "her" if applicable; replace with "I," "me," and "my" when praying for your own travel.

Dear God,
I come to You,
asking that Your blessing
be upon [name of loved one],

in the days [or weeks] ahead,
as he embarks
on this journey.

May Your light guide him
each day,
and rest with him
each night.

May the vessels that
carry him be protected,
and may he be blessed
with a safe voyage
and return.

May his mind,
his body,
and his spirit
be graced by You . . .
with comfort and ease,
with strength and joy,
with health and peace,
throughout his travels.

I sit with this prayer
upon my heart.
Please receive it,
oh Divine.

Amen

COPING WITH INSOMNIA

Insomnia has become more and more common in our modern lives. Various factors contribute to this. Prayer and meditation/visualization can be of great help in slowing down the chatter in our minds, and allowing us to unwind before bedtime and even during periods of sleeplessness. When lying awake at night, turn to God and create sacred space.

STONES TO USE

FLUORITE: *to quiet the chatter of the mind, to relax (use before sleep)*

SNOW QUARTZ: *to bring forth calm*

ROSE QUARTZ: *to promote self-love and calm*

MANTRAS

Please note that sometimes mantras can be energizing. It will be best to first try a mantra a few hours before you go to bed to see how you react.

MEDITATION/VISUALIZATION

(Listening to sounds of nature, such as ocean waves, can be helpful in this meditation.)

As you are lying down, close your eyes. Inhale and exhale gently. Feel a calm grow within you. Feel a tenderness of emotion enveloping you. Allow your mind to drift away into nothingness. Imagine you are near an ocean on the sand. Hear the ocean waves. Feel the breeze caress your senses. Look at the night stars in your mind's eye. Feel your body relaxing more and more, as a warm white light embraces you in a loving peace. Relax into this feeling. Allow it . . . and let go.

Oh Beloved,
I am calling You
in the hours of dark,
between night
and the awakening of dawn.

My body and mind
crave to seek refuge in sleep,
but my soul cannot find its quiet . . .

I cannot hear beyond the noise . . .
the inner chatter,
the restless tides
that crash against my inner being,
in these hours of late.

Beloved,
I turn to You to understand,
to resolve, to silence,
to accept this anxiety that fuels me,
that ignites my soul with turmoil,
that allows me no calm, no rest.

In these moments of questioning,
of yearning . . .
I wish to allow,
to hear, to embrace . . .
the cries and whispers
of the voice within me . . .

Oh God . . .
Lead me to this . . .
as I sit in communion with You,
in this sacred space of being.

I know through this . . .
the chatter will quiet,
and there,
I will envision the white clouds
drifting above me . . .
upon the vastness of Your blue skies
and shining stars . . .

My heavy eyelids shall close,
as my body relaxes into sweet slumber,
drifting into this loving space of being . . .
dreaming joyously,
resting in the sublime calm
of Your loving embrace,
as deep sleep envelops me . . .

FOR EMPATHY

An important step in healing our world is to be kinder, more compassionate, and more united. To do this, we need to develop greater empathy. Let us open our hearts to one another. Let us try to see and understand one another's pain, and always see through the eyes of Love.

MANTRAS

"We are one, of the same cloth, of Love"

OM MANI PADME HUM: *to invoke compassion*

OM AH HUM: *to embrace the Universal vibrations of the Infinite*

OM AMI DEVA HRIH: *to bring forth compassion*

ONG SO HUNG: *to open our hearts to the light within us*

ASHEM VOHU: *to connect to the light within as we
    connect to the light of All*

Dear Beloved,
I wish to open my eyes,
so I may see others
in all their beauty . . .

I wish to see
from the place of light
where You reside . . .
with no judgment or
prejudice,
only love
and acceptance.

Spirit,
help me open my mind,
so I may understand
another's story.

Help me open my heart,
so I may feel another's pain.

Help me gain more wisdom
as I grow in years,
so I can better lift
another in need.

Guide me,
oh God,
so I may always
live in the purity and goodness
that I carry in my heart.

Guide me
so I may grow
in kindness,
in understanding
and compassion.

Guide me so I may always
remember
that we are made
of the same cloth . . .
part of the same tapestry of life.

Oh Light,
help me remember
always,
that we are one,
and made by One.

This
I embrace.

TO HEED OUR CALLING

Many people struggle to find their life's higher calling and purpose. While it may take time to discover such truths, the answer lies in the whisper of the soul—beneath the surface of human thought and emotion, beneath the stress and pressures of everyday life. To uncover our calling, we must release our judgment of ourselves and allow time to be alone in silence and meditation, making way for the light of our truth.

STONES TO USE

FLUORITE: *to awaken us to our dreams*

AMETHYST: *to open us to the channels of communication*

ROSE QUARTZ: *to open us to self-love*

CARNELIAN: *to honor the self*

LAPIS LAZULI: *to see with higher wisdom and truth*

MANTRAS

"Reveal to me Thy truth"

SATANAMA: *to come to the understanding of our life and its deeper meaning*

SO HUM/HAM SA: *to connect to the breath*

ONG SO HONG: *to open the heart's energy*

Mangala Charan Mantra (see appendix A)

Chant the name of the Divine, in any way that you wish

MEDITATION

(OPTIONAL: FLAME MEDITATION WITH THE USE OF A CANDLE)

Breathe in gently and exhale. Let your mind find its calm. Be loving to yourself and release all judgment. Allow your mind to enter vastness. Remain in this space. Put your hand on your heart and feel it

beating. Honor yourself and sit in the quiet of your being. Allow your
heart to open and embrace the light: the miraculous silence.

Oh Beloved,
I cannot hear the whisper
of my restless soul . . .
I know not
the higher purpose
of my steps
here on Earth.

Please guide me,
dear God,
to this revelation
of my calling.

I pray to find
why I have come,
where I am to be,
and where I am to journey . . .

I pray to live
with purpose,
with the knowledge
of my deeper truth.

God,
show me,
lead me
to the path
within me . . .

beneath the veils and walls,
beneath the clouds
of thoughts and fears . . .

Take me,
carry me,
deliver me
to the heart
of me . . .
to the heart of love,
to the seed of my being.

I come to You,
oh Spirit,
in search of this . . .
of the quiet,
the space within me
that will unfold
my truth to me.

This is my prayer,
dear God,
as I sit in stillness,
at Your door,
awaiting Your guidance,
awaiting *me*.

GRATITUDE FOR SPIRITS
WHO GUIDE OUR WAY

The thread that connects this realm to the afterlife is a thin one. The spirits of those who have passed remain with us and protect us, guiding our way.

Angels of light,
we bow to you,
grateful
for your guidance
and love . . .

Oh Spirits,
your faces
both known
and unfamiliar,
young
and old,
carry the love of the Divine.

You light our way,
in times of darkness.
When we are wounded,
you lift us
and caress us,
healing us,
with your loving embrace.

You let us know,
through a breeze,

a whisper,
a dream,
that you are here . . .
that we are never alone.

You travel . . .
the distance of stars and moons,
from the realms of the beyond,
through the blue skies
and unto this earth.

You come to us,
bringing messages
through our dreams
and giving us signs
of reassurance
and guidance
when awake.

In times of distress,
we feel your warm embrace,
and in times of joy,
we feel your love.

How blessed are we
to be connected to you . . .
Grateful eternally
for your endless gifts,
for your efforts,
for always remembering us.

From this,
we take strength.
We find peace
in the knowledge
that you are
within our reach,
looking over us,
always . . .

Humbly,
we sit
and bow in prayer,
chanting . . .
Namaste
Shokran
Amen

FOR A LOVED ONE IN
THE SPIRIT WORLD

Praying and speaking to loved ones who have passed on can be a source of great comfort, joy, and love. Remember that we can still connect to them. no matter how long ago they transitioned into the spirit world. They will always remain in our hearts.

My beautiful [name of spirit],
can you hear me?
Are you close by?

I call upon you today,
to tell you
that I miss you so.

I miss you
every day . . .
your face,
your voice,
your words,
your demeanor.

Although you are no longer
among us in physical form,
I know,
in the depth of my heart,
that you remain by my side,
and always will.

My dear [name of spirit],
I wish to see you
in my dreams
when I lay down to sleep.
I wish to feel your presence
when I am awake.
I wish to feel you,
to get a sign,
that you are here . . .

I pray that you have resolved
your earthly challenges,

that you are joyful,
I pray that you are at peace . . .

I know you are with God,
in His loving embrace.
I know you are with those you love,
in the realms beyond . . .

I ask that you be my guiding light
for the years I have remaining
here on Earth . . .
until the day
when we shall unite
once again.

I bow in gratitude,
for the gift
of your love.

This,
I cherish.

Namaste

GRATITUDE FOR ALL GREAT SPIRITS

*Many messengers of the Light have come before us to pave the way
toward enlightenment for humanity, and many more messengers are yet*

to come. In this prayer, we pause to express our deep appreciation and honor these great teachers.

Oh dear sisters and brothers,
you who have paved the way for our journey
toward enlightenment . . .

Each of you
has been a voice of
truth and knowledge.

Each of you
has been a light,
so that we could
see more clearly,
so that we too,
could elevate
in heart and mind,
and walk into the space of divine grace.

For all those
who have come before us—
the prophets,
teachers,
sages,
philosophers,
and poets
who were seekers of divine truth—
your beings are part of
a chain linked directly
to our existence.

Through your breath,
came the truth . . .
that which we breathe.

Through your trials,
we have learned,
and through your teachings,
we have expanded our knowledge,
and through each of your lives
we have gotten a glimpse
of the face of God . . .

For all those who are yet to come—
the children of the Light,
the messengers of Truth—
we honor you.

May your journey be graced.
May your teachings
be received with openness.
And may you be a light
for all humanity,
for the world at large . . .

With each step you take,
may you bring the world closer
to divine truth,
and may each of you carry
God's face
on and in
your heart.

To all you beautiful beings of Light—
those who were
and those who are yet to come—
we hold you in a deep embrace.

We pray for your spirits
to be in eternal joy and peace,
and we bow to you
in gratitude.

Our hearts fill
with appreciation,
as we sit,
humbly,
in your light.

Namaste

ACCEPTING THE CYCLE OF LIFE

*In trying to understand and accept the cycle of life, we can slowly begin
to release our fear of death and, in its place, find peace in the knowledge that our spirits never die.*

MANTRAS

SO HUM/HAM SA: *to connect to the breath of being*

SATANAMA: *to connect to the cycle of birth, life, death, and
rebirth, to release deep fears*

SATNAM: *to connect with your higher truth*

Judaic Mantra for Fear (see appendix A)
YA HAYY O YA HAQQ: *to call onto the truth of the Divine*
Chant the name of the Divine, in any way that you wish

We come into this world,
dear Spirit,
never fully understanding
why we are here.

We live questioning
so much of the journey . . .
the ups and downs,
the trials and triumphs.

We die many deaths
before we go;
we shed many tears,
and sometimes,
we cannot see our way . . .

We live, we love,
we experience heartache . . .

We grow, we learn, we age;
we gain and lose
family and friends . . .

This cycle of birth, life, death,
and rebirth
is a mystery to us,
one that we can never fully grasp.

What awaits us?
How do we transcend?

We are afraid of this unknown,
of what happens beyond this world,
of letting go of this earth
and all our attachments,
of our final moments . . .

Grant us faith, oh Spirit,
for we cannot always understand
the Infinite,
understand the makeup of our being.

Help us accept this cycle
and understand
that it is the reason
why we are here—
to elevate in thought
and heart,
and become
more complete.

Help us understand
that what awaits us,
when our time has come,
is Heavenly Love
and Light,
a joy and peace profound,
and our departed loved ones,
on the other side.

Help us understand
that there is nothing to fear,
that we are never alone,
for You are with us always.

Help us connect
with our higher selves,
so we may remember
that there is no *death*,
but only another chapter
of *life*.

This is our prayer . . .
to behold this mystery . . .
to accept and embrace it . . .
as we bow,
to Your infinite grace.

A NEW CHAPTER OF LIFE

*Transitional times—when one chapter ends and another begins—are
a significant and powerful period in a person's life and can take a while
to process emotionally. Often it is only afterward that we can see our
growth and appreciate all we have learned from the experience. Patience
and allowance are key, as we embrace the next step.*

Dear God,
I am neither here,
nor there.

I am at the end of a chapter
and almost,
at the beginning of a new one.

I know not how
this chapter will end,
nor how the other will begin.

I am almost at the top of a hill,
not knowing what lies
on the other side.

I know not why
my emotions feel so complicated;
I feel a restless angst within me.
And yet my soul is excited
at such unraveling!

I remember not
when I felt this way before.
It is foreign to me,
and yet I know,
it is a part of my life,
my growth.

Oh God,
as I transition to this new phase,
leaving an old one behind,
please guide me
to the pathway of knowledge,

to the understanding
of the webs I have weaved
in the tapestry of my life.

May I always see the truth,
of *me*;
may I have the vision
to follow the quests that lay
upon my heart,
that lay upon my being.

God,
grant me patience,
so I can embrace the unknown
that is upon me.

As I sit in Your light,
I know soon,
I will be there . . .
soon,
the new chapter
will commence.

Until then,
I will sit,
I will walk,
I will stand in Your light,
gazing at the vast terrain before me,
as the sun pours in
and the hours of passage begin.

With this
I await the splendor,
as I sit,
in Your embrace.

GIVING THANKS

This prayer can be read on any day (including holidays, such as Thanks-
giving) as we open our hearts and sit humbly in gratitude. The gift of
life and the endless blessings of God are upon us every day, always.

Blessed is each moment
for the gift of life
is upon us,
and thus
the gift of divine love.

Blessed is each breath,
for through this we intertwine
with the miracle
of God.

Blessed are we,
for our hearts can feel
an array of emotions
and the magic of love.

Blessed are we,
for we can think

and find resolution
in times of distress.

Blessed are we,
for each part of our bodies,
be it broken or not,
is a part of God,
and thus,
a divine gift.

Blessed are we,
for we have food
to fuel us,

and shelter,
to shield us from harm.

Blessed are we,
for we have faith,
which nourishes our souls.

Blessed is each day,
for we can rejoice
in the wonders of our world.

Blessed are we,
for we have loved.
Blessed are we . . .

And now . . .
As we journey on,
help us make decisions with clarity
and in good conscience,
dear God,
grant us compassion and kindness.
Let us remember those in need and distress,
and let us be the hand that lifts them . . .

Fill our hearts with Your love,
and with love for one another . . .
May this be the bond
that always unites us.

Help us live in the light of hope
and in the peace of grace . . .

Help us walk kindly on this earth
and respect all her creatures.

Today,
let us remember all who have come before us
who have guided our way . . .
all who have supported us,
all who have loved and nurtured us.

Dear Light of lights,
guide us on this journey
as one.

In the spirit of love and goodness,
we give You thanks.

In gratitude,
we sit.

Amen

WE ARE THE CHANGE

*Read this at times when you feel you have little say in the world
around you. Remember, the power to create change lies within each one
of us.*

MANTRAS

"We are the change" (or passages of your choice from the prayer)
"We are the breath of God"

Dear brothers and sisters,
as we sit and await
what fate may bring to our doorsteps,
we are fearing for our children and elders,
we are questioning our governments and their decisions.

It is time.

It is time for each of us to emerge,
to find within ourselves the light
that brightens even the darkest of nights.

It is through our faith and belief
in the power of the goodness and love
which exists within each being,
that we can conquer the darkness of anxiety
that the world is feeling.

Let us pray, let us meditate:
Peace can prevail.

In our meditations, thoughts, and words,
let us speak through love, not anger . . .
through tolerance, not prejudice . . .
through hope, not despair.

It is time.

It is time for us to learn from the hand of history,
honoring the spirits who have paved the way for us.
It is time for our children to know
that we, as a people,
have the power to create change
that is not derived from greed or violence.

It is time for our eyes to see the truth,
our lips to speak the truth,
and our actions to live the truth.

It is time for us to carry our faith
in our hearts,
in our steps,
and in our lives.

Let us illuminate through strength,
through compassion,
through love.

It is time . . .
let us believe in ourselves.

We are children of the Light.
We are messengers of peace.
We are the change.

PRAYER FOR ALL

We are all interconnected through divine love. Praying for the plight of other beings that we share our world with connects us more deeply with one another and with God's healing light. When one of us heals, we all heal.

MANTRAS
"We are one"
"We are of One"
"We are the children of God, the children of Light"
OM MANI PADME HUM: *to invoke compassion*
ASHEM VOHU: *to understand our connection to All*
LA ILLAHA ILLAH HU: *to see only God*
OM AMI DEVA HRIH: *to evoke compassion*
Chant the name of the Divine, in any way that you wish

MEDITATION/VISUALIZATION
(OPTIONAL: "FLAME MEDITATION" WITH THE USE OF A CANDLE)
As you breathe in and out, find your center and calm. Imagine everyone in the world sitting in a circle, under rays of light, each person holding the hand of another. Feel the love. Feel the hope. Feel the synergy of peace and joy. Embrace it and be with it.

I pray for the man
who sits on the cold pavement
with barely a shirt . . .
May Your love warm his body
on cold winter nights.

I pray for the child
who sleeps under the bridge
near the swamp . . .
May Your angels of light
wrap him in the warmth
of a mother's embrace.

I pray for the woman
who cannot see her way in the fog . . .
May You give her a cane made of hope,
so she may slowly find her way.

I pray for the sick young man
with no name,
alone in a hospital bed . . .
May he know
You are always sitting with him,
never leaving his side.

I pray for the person
whose mind resides in turmoil or confusion . . .
may she be granted the peace and clarity
to withstand her hours of darkness.

I pray for those at war,
as they witness the unspeakable each day . . .
May they know that thousands
are praying for their safe return.

I pray for those who are hungry,
without food or water . . .

May Your rains pour abundance
onto their land,
and may they feast
on the blessings of the earth.

I pray for those who have lost
faith and hope . . .
May You lead them
to the light within,
as they find their way
back to You.

I pray for those grieving
in the wake of a tragedy . . .
May You grant them
patience and fortitude
as they walk this trying journey.

I pray for all creatures
who are harmed each day . . .
May You grant us the vision
to treat them only
with kindness and respect.

I pray for all beings,
young and old,
man and woman,
human and not,
big and small,
who inhabit this earth . . .
May we all treat one another with care.

I pray
for Your waters
and the earth,
Your jungles vast,
deserts endless,
mountains strong . . .
May we tread gently upon them
and respect their place
in the Universe.

I pray . . .
May we all see You
and know we are never alone.

May we understand
that You always lift us.

May we have faith
that no matter how difficult
today, tomorrow, or the days that follow may be,
once we know You and surrender,
we will always reside
in the peaceful light of Your love.

This is my prayer for all.
And with this,
I shall remain
each day.

Shokran . . . Amen

frequently
asked questions
and references

meditation

*Meditation is silence. Silence is God In
His Infinity's Smile.*

—Sri Chinmoy

To obtain a clear and peaceful mind, it is important to integrate meditation into our daily lives. Meditation is a holistic discipline, a technique to achieve a higher state of awareness and consciousness. It relaxes the body and allows the mind to let go of distractive patterns of thought and just "be," helping us to concentrate, focus, and experience true serenity. At the pinnacle of meditation, we can achieve a state of bliss, as we connect to our higher self and, ultimately, to Source.

There are many forms of meditation. Here we will concentrate on a basic style of meditation that originated in India. This is probably the most popular form used in the United States and many other regions of the world.

WHY SHOULD I MEDITATE?

Meditation encourages us to live a richer, more enlightened existence, with greater mental clarity and peace of mind as it connects us to the realm of the Divine and our inner core. Further, it accomplishes what working out or eating healthy cannot solely achieve: it creates a balance of body, mind, and spirit. This balance supports us to live a life more free from anxiety, fear, and depression, while aiding the body in achieving better overall health (such as lowering blood pressure, improving digestion, decreasing headaches, etc.).

WHAT DOES MEDITATION ACHIEVE?

The once-distracted mind achieves balance, silence, clarity, and focus. A meditative mind gives each aspect of life its full attention, thus allowing all channels of a person's life to flow naturally.

For example, if you meditate before going to work or school, you will slowly see your performance become more focused and effective. Therefore, you will not only get more quality work done but, more important, you will do it with ease and peace. This peaceful effortlessness will extend to your marriage, relationships, children, creativity, work, and health. Meditation is to the soul what food is to the body: it is the fuel that energizes us.

HOW DOES ONE MEDITATE?

1. POSITION AND POSTURE: The best and easiest way to start meditation is to find a comfortable sitting position. For those who cannot sit comfortably, put a cushion behind or under you, or try to lie down or stand. Keep your spine as straight as you can and turn your palms upward. Close your eyes, or if you prefer to have your eyes half-shut or open, do what comes naturally to you.

2. **DISTRACTIONS AND CONDITIONING THE MIND:**
Even before you begin meditating, you may feel your mind shifting and getting restless. This is normal and natural. Constant distractions are part of how we conduct our lives in modern-day society. Concerns about work and career, family and relationships, finances and security, etc., consume our thought patterns. To train the mind to embrace stillness takes practice, concentration, and patience. In time, your mind will slowly become more quiet. Do not try to stop your thoughts or "push them out," for this can make you more anxious. Instead, imagine placing a distractive thought in an imaginary river and watch it wash away, or give it to the winds to carry.

Also, do not stress yourself by judging how well you think you are meditating. Remember, the goal of meditation is to be less stressed and more in touch with your inner core. Even practitioners who have been meditating for decades have moments when it is more challenging to concentrate. *Nonjudgment* of the self is imperative for a rewarding practice.

3. **THE PRACTICE:** Once you are in a comfortable position, become aware of your breathing. Breath is our sacred vessel—a most powerful healer—because it is through the act of breathing that we absorb and process all our experiences and release all our pent-up feelings and thoughts.

Breathe through your nose if you can. (I have a deviated septum, so if you are like me or have difficulty breathing through your nose for other reasons, breathe through your mouth.) Breathe in and out. Do not force the breath: allow it. Next, fully inhale and hold your breath for four counts. Then exhale for a duration of four counts. Your mind may still be wandering. This is okay—again, do not judge it—just continue breathing and counting slowly.

Now deepen your breathing and increase the length of your inhalations and exhalations: take eight counts to inhale, hold your breath for eight counts, then exhale for a duration of eight counts. Become more aware of your breath and its connection to the release of energy in your body. Slowly work your way to twelve or more counts, and continue to breathe until you have a sense of "letting go."

Soon your mind and body will start to relax, as you continue to breathe in and out, slow and steady. (No need to count at this point.) You may experience a tingling hot or cool sensation. This is natural. Soon after, you may feel your mind entering a state of vast nothingness. Embrace it and sit with it as long as you comfortably can. Start at five minutes a day and slowly build to twenty. Your mind will gradually get used to this pattern of relaxation and this state of "silent being."

WHAT IS THE PROCESS OF MEDITATION?

As you meditate in the way just described, you are likely to find that the process unfolds in four basic stages (although you might not reach number four in every meditation).

1. Relax in your chosen position; concentrate on your breathing.

2. Distractions may come in; don't judge them. Allow them to "drift down the river" or "be carried away by the wind," as suggested.

3. The mind achieves a more calm and relaxed meditative state as thoughts and distractions greatly diminish. You slowly become more comfortable embracing a relaxed state of *being*.

4. You experience a deep sense of elation and peace; you feel a strong connection to your higher self and, ultimately, the Universe and Source.

Again, you may not fully achieve all four stages fully during every meditation. This is okay. Embrace the process, do not judge yourself, and continue the practice.

IS MEDITATION FOR EVERYONE? IF SO, WHY IS IT SOMETIMES HARD TO DO?

I believe meditation is integral to our overall well-being, just like eating healthy and sleeping. Yet I've had many students through the years express to me that it is difficult for them to sit and concentrate and that meditation is not for them. I remind them that they have to start out gently and be disciplined about doing it every day. They can't try it for a week and then abandon the practice. This is a new type of conditioning that takes time to fully embrace. It may take a month or longer to "get in the groove" and really begin to feel comfortable with it. Do not give up on yourself and this amazing discipline!

Meditation is not unlike physical exercise. It can feel like a chore to get your workout done, but once you commit to it and begin to see results, you actually look forward to working out and continuing that practice. It's the same with meditation.

Also, many people resist sitting quietly with themselves for they fear that something unpleasant might be uncovered that will upset them or make them uncomfortable. If this is a concern, then you need to ask yourself, "What am I running from?" or perhaps more important, "Why am I running from myself?" Remember this: even your very worst fears and anxieties are safe in the space of meditation, for one of its purposes is to create a calm and loving space for you. This practice will never make you worse—only more aware of what needs to be released or embraced, thus bringing forth a deeper connection to your inner joy and harmony.

Once meditation becomes a regular practice, you will see that it is one of the best therapies for the mind and soul. Through the splendor of meditation—the focus and the breath—we release what does not serve us, and the ten or twenty minutes you spend in meditation each day will be returned to you one-hundred-fold. In fact, most practitioners find it quite enjoyable; a delicious dessert for the soul, minus the excess calories!

WHEN IS THE BEST TIME TO MEDITATE?

Mornings or late evenings are great times to meditate. Early in the day the mind is ready to focus and will embrace the relaxed concentration of meditating. Late at night the mind is ready to release the activities of the day and will welcome this quiet state. You may decide to meditate both in the morning and at night. This will enhance your well-being, as you face the day *and* night with more clarity, peace, and happiness.

The only time it is not optimal to meditate is when the stomach is full. This is true for any form of exercise, and meditation is exercise for the mind. With a full stomach, the body and mind are more lethargic and therefore not in an optimal state for meditation.

HOW OFTEN SHOULD I MEDITATE?

I recommend that you meditate every day, even if only for five minutes. Daily meditation is very different from meditation done once a week or once in a while. Training our minds to de-clutter takes *consistent* practice. Daily meditation achieves wonderful blessings for the body, mind, and spirit. To do it once in a while is like giving a hungry person half a loaf of bread. The mind and spirit are hungry to sit in this quiet space and will only feel nourished when they are fed daily.

CAN YOU EXPLAIN SOME OF THE OTHER COMMON FORMS OF MEDITATION?

FLAME (OR OBJECT) MEDITATION: In this form of meditation, we concentrate on the flame of a candle while inhaling and exhaling. This works beautifully for many because concentrating the eyes on an external object allows the mind to narrow into focus. Soon we become unaware of the candle and settle into a meditative state. Alternatively, some focus their attention on an object (object meditation) for similar results.

WALKING MEDITATION: This meditative technique is deeply rooted in Native American and Buddhist traditions.

As we concentrate on the motion of our steps when we walk, we release blockages and anxieties through our breath and body, and our mind becomes more clear and focused. With each step we become more immersed in the movement and walk further away from our inner chatter and chaos.

OTHER POPULAR FORMS: Visualization and mantras are popular practices among meditators and seekers. Please refer to the sections on these practices in the table of contents.

Additionally, dancing, playing an instrument, drawing, and chanting are a few different channels to achieve a meditative state through the concentrated immersion into the activity.

CAN MEDITATION HELP WITH OCD, DEPRESSION, AND ANXIETY?

Yes. Meditation has been an aspect of Eastern medicine for centuries, and today Western medicine also recommends this practice to support treatment of phobias, obsessive behavior, depression, and anxiety. The beauty of this practice is that it does not cost any money and can be done anywhere, at any time, at any age. The application is simple, the discipline is healing, and the rewards are life changing.

CAN WE MEDITATE ON A SPECIFIC THOUGHT?

Yes. We can meditate on a subject, an issue, or a challenge, with the intention of receiving new insight and awareness. After we have meditated, we can often see the subject with more clarity and resolve any dilemmas we may have regarding it. In my classes, I usually guide students to meditate on a specific subject that has been upsetting them. Through breathing and focused intention, they generally experience release and a sense of liberation from whatever discord they may have felt.

CAN WE MEDITATE FOR OTHERS IN AN AREA OF THE WORLD WHERE THERE HAS BEEN UNREST OR TRAGEDY?

Yes! When part of the world is at war, or there's been a natural disaster or tragic event, we can meditate for those affected, either by ourselves or in a group setting. Throughout the meditation, we can imagine healing white light around the affected region. The pure healing power of these meditations can shift negative thoughts and patterns beyond what we are able to see. That is why many traditions do group meditations. (I have conducted many such meditations in my classes for this purpose.)

> *Meditation will give you a stronger connection to your divine inner being and to God. It will enlighten you on every level, and harmonize your body, mind, and spirit as it aligns you with your deeper purpose. As you embrace this practice, pure wonder and magic for the soul will unfold for you. This is the splendor of meditation.*

visualization

*Visualize this thing that you want, see
it, feel it, believe in it. Make your mental
blueprint, and begin to build.*

—ROBERT COLLIER

Visualization is the practice of consciously forming specific positive mental images to support or bring forth an intention. This can be as simple as planting an image in your mind or imagining active scenes of you and your life as if you are watching a movie. Visualization can be done as a separate practice or easily integrated into prayer or meditation.

The main ingredient of visualization is the power of the imagination—to create images that will ultimately lead us to the altar of new perceptions, transformation, growth, and healing. Visualization can be therapeutic in aiding us to break through our limitations and challenges and find belief in the self.

WHY SHOULD I PRACTICE VISUALIZATION?

The three main purposes of visualization are as follows:

1. TO QUIET THE MIND: As an aid to meditation or a
   more calm emotional state, you might visualize
   relaxing nature scenes or healing white light.
2. THERAPEUTIC: If you feel trepidation about a
   particular issue or activity (such as public speaking or
   flying), you might reduce or even eliminate your
   anxiety by visualizing positive images that help to
   reframe your perceptions.
3. TO MATERIALIZE AN INTENTION: When you desire a
   particular outcome for yourself or another, you might
   visualize steps to bring forth your intention.

Through regular practice, visualization can guide us into the
realm of our true dreams and wishes, greatly reduce our fears, and
support positive thinking and affirmations.

HOW DO I PRACTICE VISUALIZATION?

There are three approaches to visualization practice that I recommend:

1. AFFIRMATION VISUALIZATION: This is an anytime/
   anywhere approach in which you essentially visualize
   an affirmation or intention. For example, if you feel
   anxious about flying and you are about to board a
   plane, you might take a moment to "affirm" that all is
   well and you are safe, as you visualize the plane as a
   beautiful white bird gracefully and safely carrying you
   through the sky to your destination.

This type of visualization requires no prior mental setup and no structured meditation setting. You simply hold the image in your mind with your eyes open or closed (although closing your eyes is preferred since you can more fully immerse yourself in the imagery).

2. CREATIVE VISUALIZATION: In this approach, you set aside a few minutes to focus on a specific visual sequence. Let's say you're a musician and you want to mentally prepare for an upcoming performance. You might take a few moments to ease into a meditative state by counting breaths. Once relaxed, you would visualize yourself successfully performing onstage, either from the perspective of the audience (movie-style) or through your own eyes. With creative visualization, the idea is to liberate yourself from your mental or emotional barriers and imagine the most positive outcome. Also, creative visualization flows naturally into meditation and vice versa.

3. OPEN-FLOW VISUALIZATION: This is where you allow your mind to sit in vastness and quiet and just flow with whatever scenes or images happen to appear. This allows the inner door of your spirit to be opened as you bask in the desires of the soul, expressed through the imagery shown to you.

Note: Use of colorful imagery and nature/ambient recordings can further enhance your visualization practice.

IS VISUALIZATION THE SAME AS DAYDREAMING?

No, not exactly. Daydreaming tends to be more fantasy driven: in daydreams we usually indulge ourselves in the pleasurable feelings of an event playing out in our mind. Daydreaming is a welcome break from our daily activities. As a young teenager, I used to daydream about meeting pop star David Cassidy. I never seriously thought it would happen; I just enjoyed the fantasy of it! Daydreams do not usually play a part in serious expectations of manifesting an intention.

In visualization, we intend a specific, positive effect. We hold certain images in our mind with the intention that they will either be made manifest or will support us in achieving a more empowered state of mind.

IS VISUALIZATION A GOOD TOOL FOR PHOBIAS, FEARS, AND ANXIETY?

Yes. Visualization can be very effective for any of the above. The mind is a powerful healer, and through visualization, limitations and restrictions are often dissolved into new visions of our reality. As we move away from negativity and fear, we find the doors open to positive thoughts and newfound beliefs. It's a wonderful way to help release patterns that do not serve the soul. (However, if the root of the phobia, fear, or anxiety is especially deep, please consult with a practitioner.)

CAN WE VISUALIZE FOR THE BENEFIT
OF THE WORLD?

Yes! Just as in certain meditation practices where we concentrate on a desired intention for world peace or healing for a particular region of the world, we can do this with visualization. An effective visualization technique is to see the healing taking place in ideal conditions. We can also visualize healing white light embracing the region or the world at large. This is a beautiful visualization!

HOW CAN VISUALIZATION HELP IF WE ARE
GOING THROUGH SOMETHING VERY
DIFFICULT AND AN UNDESIRED OUTCOME
SEEMS INEVITABLE?

There are many instances in which we cannot change an outcome but can see it in a different light and experience it with less resistance. For example, let us say a loved one is transitioning from this life. In our visualizations, we can see him or her surrounded by light or even among a "greeting group" of loved ones from the spiritual realm. We can also visualize that we are embracing them and telling them how much we love them. After their transition, we can see them as beings of light, free of pain, and even as our guardian angels, happily guiding us here on the earthly plane. This creative visualization will allow us a new perception of the transition and bring forth a more peaceful acceptance of a difficult situation.

CAN MUSIC OR CERTAIN SOUNDS AID US IN VISUALIZATION?

Yes. Music is a wonderful "opener of channels" and can lend an important inspirational or ambient component to the visualization of a particular intention. Also, sounds of nature—either recorded or as an actual background to your session—can support visualization.

CAN VISUALIZATION HELP US MANIFEST OUR DREAMS?

Visualization helps transform limited thought patterns and perceptions because it ultimately guides and inspires us to take positive action to create a more fulfilling reality in our lives. However, this does not mean that visualization creates unfounded magic! Let us say, for example, I am fifty years old and have a dream of winning the Nobel Prize in Literature. I visualize myself being awarded the prize but haven't actually done much work on the craft of writing. This would be a visualization that can't find its seed in the reality of my life. However, a visualization that I find my calling and my peace, and have a life that is fulfilling, is one that is possible for each of us.

> *Visualization awakens us to new possibilities, as our old mind-set shifts and the door to our innermost hopes and dreams magically opens.*

mantra

*Mantra is the oar of the boat; it is the
instrument you use to cross the samsara
of your restless mind, with its unending
thought waves. The mantra can also be
compared to a ladder that you climb to
reach the heights of God-realization.*

—AMMA

A mantra is a repeated word, phrase, or passage that awakens the soul to self-realization. Mantra—which translates from ancient Sanskrit as "instrument of the mind"—is viewed as a transformative practice. The vibrational resonance of a mantra connects us to the seed of the soul and the Divine, and helps to remove all residue and limitations from our being.

WHEN AND WHERE DID MANTRAS ORIGINATE?

While it is impossible to trace the exact point of origin, we can only presume that from the time there were spoken words, there was some form of mantra. We know that the Vedic tradition brought forth mantra as part of Hindu spiritual practice about three thousand years ago. Mantras have also been vital in many other traditions, including Sikhism, Jainism, and Buddhism. The Dalai Lama states, "Without depending upon mantra, Buddhahood cannot be attained."

In the Christian and Judaic faiths, a passage from the Old or New Testaments, or the name of the Divine, can be used as a mantra. In the Gospel according to John, it is written, "In the beginning was the word. And the word was with God, and the word was God," thus acknowledging the significance of word and sound. And in the Islamic and Sufi traditions, mantras (known as *zikr*) are often repeated as chants hundreds of times.

HOW DO I SELECT A MANTRA?

A mantra is selected based on your soul's desire: What are you yearning for? Are you seeking a deeper connection to Source? What might you need to become aware of? What's been holding you back that you would like to release?

Once you've defined your intention, there are two basic options in selecting a mantra:

FIND AN EXISTING ONE: Whether you do some research online or get a suggestion from someone experienced with mantra practice, there are literally hundreds of choices available (see appendix A for a partial list of options). In some cases, a spiritual practitioner can assign a specific mantra to you.

Note: In Hindu and Buddhist traditions, there is a vast selection of specific mantras for various intentions.

CREATE YOUR OWN: If there is a particular word, phrase, or passage that especially resonates with you and your chosen intention, use it! There are no set rules for what you can use as a mantra. You may even choose a phrase from a song or a brief but inspiring passage from a book. (It's interesting how often a mantra might find *you*.)

A student of mine created his own mantra—"I wish to release my deep inner fear"—and would recite it each morning for eleven minutes as part of his daily meditation. He did this for two months and eventually he did, in fact, feel his deep inner fears cleansed from his soul. The special connection he had with his mantra supported his healing process.

IS IT BETTER TO CHOOSE A MANTRA WITH FAMILIAR OR UNFAMILIAR LANGUAGE?

There are two schools of thought on this subject. Many believe that reciting an ancient mantra (comprised of unfamiliar language) can be the most transformational, for in not knowing the words we do not link them to any particular experience. This gets us "out of our head" and allows the words and the sound waves to unlock the doorways of our being. Others feel more comfortable reciting a mantra in words they understand, because of the familiarity they have with them. I have found both to be effective in my own practice, as well as those of my students.

DOES A MANTRA HAVE ONE DEFINITION OR MANY?

Although every mantra typically has a specific meaning, that meaning will take on a life of its own through practice. This is because an unveiling or unraveling process usually occurs when reciting a mantra; and as new revelations appear, deeper meanings are often revealed to us.

HOW DOES ONE PRACTICE DOING A MANTRA?

Aside from practicing in a group setting, there are two basic ways to practice on your own:

MANTRA SPECIFIC—This is a structured approach where you set aside at least three to five minutes per day for a minimum of thirty days (or whatever your mantra's tradition of origin recommends) and practice a certain mantra with a specific intention in mind.

MANTRA FLEXIBLE—With this more intuitive approach, you simply practice anytime you feel moved to.

A mantra can be practiced in a whisper, in silence, or out loud. The goal is to lose yourself in the rhythm and *sound* of the mantra, so recite your mantra as it suits you (unless instructed otherwise).

Also, if you choose to practice your mantra with a specific number of repetitions—as opposed to an overall duration of time—you might consider using mala beads (also known as prayer beads). This is a string of beads that aids you in counting the number of times you recite your mantra. You can also count with your fingers. However, as we immerse ourselves in this process, we typically lose count as we connect more deeply to the mantra.

WHAT POSTURE DO I USE?

Whenever we wish to sit with the higher self, we need to honor the space. I recommend that you sit in a comfortable position. But you could also stand, or even sway, if this helps you get more immersed in your mantra. Follow your body's natural rhythms; there are no set rules here.

What is most important is not how you do it but the purity of the intention behind it. Like prayer, doing a mantra is not about just saying the words but allowing the energy—and thus the Divine—into the landscape of our beings.

WHEN SHOULD I PRACTICE?

You can recite a mantra at any time of the day or night, incorporating it into your regular prayer or meditation time or doing it by itself. Mantras can have an energizing effect, so be sure to see how you react to them before scheduling a late-night practice. If you are practicing in a more structured way for a number of weeks, it is recommended that you create a space for the practice around the same part of each day, if possible. This will create a more disciplined practice. Once again, as with all other types of spiritual practice, it is with discipline, intention, patience, allowance, and belief that mantra will reward you tenfold.

CAN WE DO MORE THAN ONE MANTRA AT A TIME?

Yes. At spiritual or religious centers, many mantras may be recited at a gathering. However, when we are trying to work on something specific, or just develop the discipline, I feel it is best to do one mantra at a given session. This will strengthen your practice and enable you to focus more clearly on your intention.

SOMETIMES I FEEL LIKE I'M BENEFITING FROM MY MANTRA PRACTICE, WHILE AT OTHER TIMES, MY MIND WANDERS AND I DON'T FEEL CONNECTED TO THE PRACTICE. IS THIS NORMAL?

Once again, the first thing to remember about practices like mantra or meditation is not to judge yourself on how well you are "performing" them or to constantly evaluate the perceived results you are getting. As discussed in the meditation section, our minds are simply not conditioned for this type of practice, so it takes time and patience. And even then, the most experienced practitioners have difficulty concentrating all the time, so accept that it will be an ongoing journey.

Also, you may have a week or more when you feel very connected to your mantra, and then the following week you may not. This does not mean you have regressed. It's just part of the practice.

As for the results . . . be patient with yourself. In this practice, we are often addressing blockages and personal issues that are layered together in a complex web of deep thought or behavioral patterns, which create discomfort in us and do not serve our soul. This unraveling and unveiling process is not the task of one day, or one week. The soul releases these limitations when it is ready. We can caress it, coax it, and guide it, but each of us has our own inner timetable, guided by our own rhythm, and it cannot be rushed. Trust that this process will unfold for you as it is intended to.

> *As you embrace the mantra, you will reclaim yourself.*
> *And in this radiance, your soul will emerge with a*
> *clearer purpose and a deeper connection to Source as*
> *you journey forward.*

stone healing

*I believe that there is a subtle magnetism
in Nature, which, if we unconsciously
yield to it, will direct us aright.*

—Henry David Thoreau

Mother Earth is our healer, and from her we have drawn herbs and medicines that have remedied thousands of ailments. From her plants, flowers, and leaves we have further created many cures, so it is not surprising that in her precious stones (gems/crystals) we can find healing elements for our body, mind, and spirit.

Stone healing is an ancient form of balancing the body and mind through the application and usage of various gems and crystals. It can open channels to healing physical, emotional, mental, and spiritual blockages and can be used in conjunction with other practices such as prayer, meditation, and mantra.

WHAT IS THE HISTORY OF STONE HEALING?

For thousands of years, in civilizations in India, the Middle East, Africa, Greece, Asia, and North America, stones have been used to balance bodily energies and as remedies for hundreds of ailments. Many Native American tribes have traditionally revered turquoise as a "stone more precious than gold" and considered it indispensable in healing various ailments. Jade has been deeply rooted in Chinese culture for thousands of years and is used in everything from promoting emotional balance to detoxification. And rubies, known as the "king of the gemstones" in many cultures around the globe—including Hindu, African, Greek, and Roman—are renowned for benefitting the heart both as a powerful "love center opener" and as an aid to the circulatory system.

Stones have also played a historical role in conveying elevated spiritual and social status: prophets had rings of jade and agate, the Buddha is often depicted with jewelry made of precious stones, and the crowns of kings are ornate with priceless gems.

DO STONES HAVE DIFFERENT MEANINGS IN VARIOUS CULTURAL TRADITIONS AND COUNTRIES?

The definitions can vary to a degree but not totally. For example, I have been buying crystals from a Native American store for many years, and I noticed that the staff described uses for some of the stones that were a bit different from what I had learned. For example, in the Middle East, turquoise is a protective stone that wards off negative vibrations. In the Native American shop's definition, turquoise is not only a protective stone but one that brings us closer to our higher truth.

Also, bear in mind that stone healing is an intuitive practice. Each person may have a slightly different experience with a given stone. I have used amethyst for years on the throat chakra and also to support the channels to fertility, while other practitioners may use different stones for this area. Our intuition can truly guide us in the application of stones, so long as our usage remains in alignment with the general properties of the stone.

ARE STONES AND CRYSTALS THE SAME?

The main difference between stones and crystals is in their mineralization elements and molecular structure. But here we use the term "stone healing" to encompass all gems from the earth.

HOW DOES STONE HEALING WORK?

Each stone carries a different vibration, or frequency, that can be used for specific areas of healing or enhancement. I feel that stone healing is generally most effective when the stone touches the skin, therefore I generally recommend that you hold the stone in your hand. However, the vibrations of some stones can be so powerful that you can feel them even when they don't touch the skin. In those instances, you can place the stone on a nearby table or you carry it in your pocket throughout the day.

To practice stone healing effectively, however, *you must first understand the powerful properties that stones possess and get a feel for how you react and respond to a given stone*. Your body will intuitively guide you, as this can be different for each person.

Stones have always been found to be effective in *aiding and supporting pathways* to healing. Because our bodies do not always have a way to release the stress we hold on to, our pent-up anxieties, fear, anger, depression, guilt, and other emotions can manifest in aches, pains, and illnesses and also hinder us emotionally, mentally, and spiritually. The use of stones opens the channels to these specific areas and brings forth healing vibrations and energy. I have had many students say that stone healing has transformed their ability to tune in and remove the blockages that challenge them, and thus transform their lives. Once again, like the other practices in this book, it is the intention and belief behind the practice that is so critical to our healing.

Note: Stone healing is not recommended to treat an illness or to replace Western or Eastern medicine. See your practitioner for any health concerns.

WHAT IS INVOLVED IN THE PROCESS OF SELECTING AND USING A STONE?

First, you select a stone based on how its properties might positively affect a particular area of your life or challenge you want to work on. (See appendix B for more information about stones and their properties.)

Once you have acquired the stone of your choice, you'll need to "clear" it (see below), and then hold it in your hand with a light fist for a few minutes to get a feel for how your body reacts to it. Each person's response is different, so you have to gently evaluate how the energy of a given stone interacts with your personal energy and the physical energy of your body.

HOW DO I "CLEAR" A STONE?

A stone is a precious healing element of the earth and should be honored as such. Stones need to be cleared/cleansed when you acquire them, unless they were already cleared for you. There are several ways to clear a stone, including

A) putting it in a glass bowl of cool water with a pinch of sea salt for several hours;
B) holding it under cold running water for a few minutes;
C) placing it in a potted plant or burying it in the earth for a couple of days;
D) setting it in direct sunlight for several hours or under the light of a full moon for at least one night.

After you have used the stone for a given amount of time, it is recommended that you repeat this cleansing process and clear the energies. For example, if you have used the stone several times while angry, you may want to clear the stone of this energy, just to be sure it has not been drained of its properties and healing vibrations. Once you cleanse it, you can continue your normal use of it.

CAN I SHARE MY STONE WITH SOMEONE ELSE?

Stones are sacred and powerful and become a part of us through regular usage. You can give your stone to someone else once you have finished using it, as long as it has been cleared. But for two people to use a stone at the same time is not something I recommend. We each carry our own vibration, and the stone may take on and store the specific energies of each individual.

HOW MIGHT A STONE-HEALING SESSION UNFOLD?

While there are many ways to utilize stones for healing, here's an effective step-by-step process:

1. Choose the recommended stone for the desired effect—healing or help with a particular area.
2. Take off any jewelry, shut down phones and other electronics, and distance yourself from any distractions.
3. Sit or lie down. Be comfortable.
4. Hold the stone in your hand.
5. Relax, close your eyes, and tune into the vibrations.
6. Continue for several minutes or for as long as your body guides you to.
7. Once you set the stone down, remain in position and just relax for a few minutes.
8. After the session, drink a glass of water.

Once again, stone therapy is a very intuitive form of healing. As you tune into our body, it will guide you. Also, do not be concerned if you do not feel any strong vibrations. Sometimes stones work in a more subtle manner.

CAN I USE STONES IN MEDITATIONS?

Yes. Many stones are wonderful channels to further enhance our meditation practice. Stones such as amethyst, rose quartz, and fluorite are great openers to the mind and heart.

WHAT IS THE RECOMMENDED TIME AND FREQUENCY OF A STONE-HEALING SESSION?

Typically, we can feel the energy of stones anywhere from a few minutes on. I would start with five to ten minutes per stone, two or three times per week, and listen to your body to guide you from there.

Bear in mind that stone healing can be used intuitively, without a lot of structure. During a vulnerable period in my life, I used malachite and onyx daily, until I regained my inner composure and strength. I felt the stones were supporting me for that period of time. So, for example, if you are going to an important meeting and need to feel grounded and centered, you can use an onyx for that purpose.

CAN STONE HEALING BE USED IN CONJUNCTION WITH OTHER HEALING PRACTICES, SUCH AS ACUPUNCTURE, MASSAGE, ETC.?

Other healing practices can incorporate stones if the practitioners understand their properties. For example, integrating stones into certain massage therapy practices is not uncommon. However, we have to be careful not to stimulate the body with too much energy, so we must slowly integrate stone therapy with other healing mediums.

WHY HAVE YOU ONLY USED SOME STONES IN THIS BOOK?

There are over seven hundred stones and crystals. I have only introduced the more traditional ones, and the ones that I have personally worked with. If you want to know more about stones and stone healing, I have recommended a few wonderful books at the end of appendix B.

DO OUR BIRTHSTONES HAVE MORE HEALING ENERGY FOR US?

In my experience, I don't believe there is a definitive answer for this. As is the case with any stone, I believe each individual must experience their birthstone firsthand to know if it happens to have any healing properties for them.

ARE THERE ANY PRECAUTIONS ONE SHOULD TAKE WHEN PRACTICING STONE HEALING?

I do recommend being mindful of the following aspects:

1. Allow some adjustment time: Always ease into the use of any new stone. Start by using it for a few minutes at a time, and allow it to slowly do its work. Building a trusting relationship between you and these precious earth elements will ease your anxieties, as this is something new for the *body*, as well as the spirit. Also, sometimes when we focus on a specific challenge and open the channels of our healing, we may feel a bit uncomfortable at first. Once again, patience and trust will help us find our calm in the process.

2. Refrain from use late at night (unless the stone is for relaxation and sleep): You will likely feel a tangible energy with certain stones, so I don't recommend practicing in the late evening because the increased vibrations could make getting to sleep a difficult task!

3. Avoid using many stones together: Address only one or two areas of interest at a time so you can truly give them your best attention. If you focus on several areas at once, the variety of stones that would be needed may carry different vibrations, and this can send mixed energies to the body. If, for example, you want one stone to help calm your anxieties and another to give you energy, they may not work well together. Using multiple stones in your practice simply gives the body too much information, potentially overloading your receptor antennas. Instead, I would suggest using no more than two or three stones, at the most, at any given time.

4. Avoid using stones if you are pregnant or your body is under special treatment, i.e. chemotherapy, radiation, etc.: During such times it is best to consult with a practitioner who knows the properties of the stones and the particulars of your condition.

As the earth blesses us with her precious stones, we find pathways to our healing and enrichment to our daily practices. This is the gift of stone healing.

a selection of mantras

There are thousands of mantras to choose from, but the list below includes just some of the more familiar ones. While many of these mantras have crossed over into various traditions, we have listed each in the category with which it is most commonly associated.

The definitions and applications below are very general, designed to give you a basic understanding of each mantra. If you feel drawn to any of these mantras, consider doing a little research on them. A mantra has much depth and cannot adequately be defined in a word, because it goes beyond the word and into the resonance of sound and senses. This is ultimately why a mantra will unfold differently for each person.

Universal

OM/AUM: one of the most sacred syllables; the sound, and essence, of the Universe.

AMMA: the Divine Mother. Omma, Ma, Mama, Madre, and Mother may be used for Divine Mother but can also just be used as simply "mother."

ABBA: the Heavenly Father. Abu, Pa, Ba, Padre, and Father may be used for Heavenly Father but can also just be used as simply "father."

MAA BA AAH: A mantra I have partially created. "Ma" is for the Mother, "Ba" for the Father, and "Aah" for the self; this mantra connects us and anchors us to this triangle.

Buddhist

OM AH HUM: to embrace the universal vibration of the Infinite, on the seed level, as we awaken to All; can be done before the recitation of other mantras.

OM MANI PADME HUM: the embodiment of compassion; to forgive.

OM MUNI MUNI MAHAMUNI SHAKYAMUNI SVAHA: "Oh Great Wise One," to invoke enlightenment.

OM AMI DEVA HRIH: enhances and brings compassion; assists in the removal of obstacles on your path.

OM TARE TUTTARE TURE SOHA: brings forth inner peace; assists in the removal of mental, physical, or emotional blockages within the individual, and their relationships; liberates.

NAM MYOHO RENGE KYO: a multi-layered mantra that aids in understanding the intricacies of our world; helps bring clarity, rejuvenation, focus, and a confidence in being. A connector to the realm of existence.

Vedic

SO HUM: "I am that"—sound of the breath; inhale and exhale, thus connecting us to creation.

HAM SA: "I am that"—sound of the breath; inhale and exhale, thus connecting us to creation.

TAT TVAM ASI: "That thou art"; for self-realization.

OM HANSAM HANSAHA: for health protection.

OM NAMAH SHIVAYA: "I bow to the Divine Consciousness."

OM SHANTI OM: for peace.

RAMA RAMA OR RAMA RAHIM: to call to God—"Benevolent and Merciful One, he who is so kind" (Gandhi's favorite mantra).

GAYATRI MANTRA:

Aum bhoor bhuwah swaha
tat savitur varenyam
bhargo devasaya dheemahi
dhiyo ya naha prachodayat

Meaning: "To inspire our wisdom and illuminate our minds so we can journey in the path of light and righteousness."

Kundalini Thought

HAR: a call to the Creator; energizing the being and spirit.

ONG NAMO GURU DEV NAMO: calling to the higher self, "I bow to the divine wisdom, the divine teacher within."

ONG SO HUNG: opening the heart energy as we say, "I am Thou, creative consciousness."

RA MA DA SA SA SAY SO HUNG: to create healing as we call to "All that there is." Many believe this mantra supports our wishes.

WAHE GURU: to elevate our being as we call to the Divine.

SATNAM: "I am truth"; can help release uncomfortable feelings when recited slowly.

SATANAMA: to release thought as we chant "birth, life, death, rebirth" and connect to the seed of our being. Also releases blockages and brings forth confidence.

Aad guray nameh
jugaad guray nameh
sat guray nameh
siri guru devay nameh

A four-passage mantra recited for the protection of Light; "to bow to the wisdom of ages as we bow to the great Unseen Wisdom."

Judaic
YAHWEH, ADONAI, OR ELOHIM: name of the Divine
SHALOM: "Peace"
YISMACH MOSHE B'MATNAT CHELKO: recited to help with anxiety and self-worth.

FOR HEALING (AND FEAR)
B'yado afkid ruchi,
b'eit ishan, v'aira, v'im ruchi geviyati,
Adonai li v'lo ira

Meaning: "Into the hands of God,
I entrust my spirit, asleep or awake,
spirit and body, God is with me, I will not fear."

FOR GRATITUDE
Zeh hayom asah Adonai,
nagila v'nism'cha vo

Meaning: "God made this day; let us rejoice."

Christianity

MARANATHA: Aramaic, to call to the Divine.

HALLELUJAH: "Praise to God."

"PEACE BE WITH YOU"

HAIL MARY

THE LORD'S PRAYER: "Our Father who art in heaven, hallowed be Thy name" (recite first line or two, or other lines, of this prayer as a mantra).

KYRIE ELEISON: "Lord have mercy" (Greek).

Islam/Sufism

BISMILLAH AL RAHMAN AL RAHIM: "In the name of God, the kind and merciful."

YA ALLAH OR ALLAH: to call to the Divine.

ALLAH O AKBAR OR ALLAH U AKBAR: "God is great."

HU OR YA HU: to call to the Beloved.

LA ILLAHA ILLA HU: "There is no one but God."

YA HAYY O YA HAQQ: "Oh life, oh Truth."

YA RAHMAN O YA RAHIM: "Oh Kind and Benevolent One"

YA SHAFFEE O YA KHAFFEE: "Oh Healer."

Zoroastrian

ASHEM VOHU: "The light of Truth within us is connected to the light of All."

Ashem vohu vashistem asti

Ushta asta, ushta ahmai

Hyat ashai vahistai ashem

The more complete version translates as, "Radiant happiness comes to those who are righteous, for the sake of righteousness alone":

HUMATA, HUKHTA, HUVARSHTA, SVAH: "Pure thoughts, pure actions, pure words, grow"; recited to create cleansing and purification.

Native American

WAKAN TANKA: "The Great Spirit" (or Great Mystery).

Hawaiian

HO'OPONOPONO: to reconcile, to forgive, and thus bring forth joy. Can also be used for reconciliation and forgiveness in relationships.

In Christianity, Judaism, Islam, and other traditions, passages from holy scriptures can be recited as mantras. These can include songs or prayers. Also, names of messengers/prophets, as well as the Divine can be chanted. Opening and ending statements such as "Peace be upon you" or "God be with you" and words such as "love," "kindness," etc., may also be recited as mantras.

I recognize that many religions and spiritual traditions in our world besides the ones listed here use some form of mantra. There are simply too many to include them all in this brief section.

I have opted to capitalize the names of the mantras to emphasize their importance.

THE FOLLOWING PASSAGES AND WORDS, SOME FROM THIS BOOK, COULD BE USEFUL AS MANTRAS:

"With your Light, I sit"

"I am the breath of love"

"I am the breath of God"

"I surrender to Thy will"

"Your will I embrace"

"I am of Love"

"I am the child of Light"

"With this, I embrace"

"I bow to your grace"

"In your light I Shall remain"

NAMASTE: "My light respects yours"

SHOKRAN: to give thanks

KHODAYA: "Oh Divine" or "Oh God"

AMEN OR AMEEN: "the Word," gratitude and thanks

RECOMMENDED WEBSITES ON MANTRA

thebuddhacenter.org

kundaliniyoga.com

synagogue3000.org

torahveda.org

prescottcircle.org

sixwise.com

soulworkwithjeni.com

treelight.com

omthathwamasi.blogspot.com

feathersandbones.blogspot.com

RECOMMENDED BOOKS ON MANTRA

The Healing Power of the Human Voice by James D'Angelo

Healing Mantras: Using Sound Affirmations for Personal Power, Creativity, and Healing by Thomas Ashley-Farrand

stone index

Please note that some of these stones come in various colors, and this can create slight variation in their proprieties. Also, as stated in the section on stone healing, different traditions and practitioners may interpret stones differently. Ultimately, our higher intuitions and body guide us to the applications and usage of stones.

AMBER: Powerful, soothing, lifts the spirits. Radiates an energy of heat and light. Aids with infection, respiratory and intestinal concerns.

AMETHYST: "The opener of channels" to creativity and communication, such as speaking and writing. Purifying, de-stressing. Promotes awareness. Wonderful to use during meditation. Aids with insomnia and headaches. Brings forth the positive energies within us, and helps us expand our inner realm.

Author's note: I have used amethyst in many of my classes to support and open blocked fertility energies.

ARAGONITE: Promotes calm in times of high stress. Opens us to new visions. Supports care and tending to the earth. Energizing.

AQUAMARINE: Good stone for traveling, especially over or around water. Helps release blockages, fears, anxieties, phobias, and stress. Soothing, calming, inspiring. Brings forth inner happiness and cultivates a state of calm.

BLOODSTONE: Used in times of battle to stop bleeding and bring forth courage. Helps with blood-related issues. Elevates strength and physical energy.

BLUE LACE AGATE: Supports the "feminine" energies of the body (i.e., fertility) and promotes good health. Has healing properties and encourages us to explore our "being" and embrace it. Fosters happiness and a calm, positive outlook.

CALCITE: Cleansing and clearing for our body and environment. Known for its healing properties and for stimulating the flow of positive energy in times of stress.

Author's note: This is a stone I have used to lift the spirit in times of emotional anguish and depression.

CARNELIAN: Known as the "all-around stone." Energizing and protective, empowering and self-motivating. Opens channels that feel stagnant. Gentle, calm energy. Supports us in taking positive actions toward our dreams.

CITRINE: Called the "merchant stone." Believed to herald good luck and fortune. Aids in self-esteem and opening the mind to new ideas. Brings forth clarity and focus. Promotes forward movement. Helps with endurance, relieves stress. Supports the digestive tract.

Author's note: I have recommended and used this stone many times for those who feel financially stuck, and have found it to be beneficial in guiding the individual toward constructive/productive action.

EMERALD: The "attraction stone." Positive for romance and relationships. Supports insight, aids us in seeing our truth, promotes openness, enhances memory.

FLUORITE: "Dream stone." Healing, protective stone that brings order to the chaos, clutter, and chatter in our minds and lives. Awakens our psychic and spiritual selves and connects us to the world of our inner dreams. Wonderful to use for relaxing or meditating. Promotes focus and concentration.

Author's note: This is a stone I love working with, for it takes us beneath the layers, to the seed of our truth.

GARNET: Energizing for the short term. Enhances mood; used to lessen depression and strengthen feelings of self-esteem, vitality, and encouragement. Stimulates positive energy vibrations. Supports hormones and menstruation.

GIRASOL QUARTZ: Powerful stone that brings forth inner happiness and optimism. Empowers supports focus, and enhances creativity.

Author's note: Another stone I absolutely love to use and recommend. Wonderful in times of stress, worry, confusion, or depression.

HEMATITE: A grounding, powerful stone that energizes the physical body. Supports in reducing severe anxiety and hysteria, bringing calm. Balances our spirit, mind, and body.

JADE: Healing, protective; fosters feelings of belonging and security. Supports marriage and relationships. Connects us to our ancestors, the Universe, the spiritual self. Promotes wisdom, as it releases ego.

Author's note: I have used different colors of jade to herald positive feelings of inner security. A wonderful stone to keep in various locations around the home.

JASPER: Powerful stone, slow and consistent. Grounding, strengthening, and protective. Supports our sense of security, and protects us from negative forces and energies.

Author's note: While this stone has many color variations—and thus, the meaning of each stone varies—this definition still applies to all variations.

LAPIS LAZULI: "The seer stone." Opens channels of insight and awakens the psychic eye to wisdom and truth. Brings clarity; an effective aid in meditation. Allows us to see the truth; brings honest communications. Can guide us in self-discovery.

MALACHITE: Known as the "balancer of all." Helps to align the spiritual/mental/emotional/physical energies of our body. Releases pent-up energy and fosters rejuvenation. Aids in recovery from exhaustion. Promotes expansion, focus, and intention.

Author's note: A stone no one should be without! Excellent to use on days when we feel unsure, vulnerable, or not present. Centering and strengthening in a calm way.

MOOKAITE (A FORM OF JASPER): Guides us to find the "right" pathways and make sound decisions. Aids in resolving problems. Aligns our being to the present while empowering us and connecting us to Source.

MOONSTONE: "Goddess stone." Supports the flow of feelings and energy. Opens our hearts to love, selflessness, compassion, and forgiveness. Works with bodily fluids, thus aiding menstruation, fertility, and childbirth.

MOSS AGATE: "Restoration stone." Healing, flowing, creative; it supports the release and removal of restrictive and limiting feelings such as anger and guilt. Brings harmony, relaxation, peace, friendliness, and positive

energies with friendships. Supports abundance
in agriculture, and aids with clearing pollutants.

OBSIDIAN: Guides us to the root of our emotional blockages
and barriers, and helps us break them down. Cleanses and
heals. Brings renewal. Supports the digestive tract.

ONYX: Grounding. Promotes focus. Supports us in
containing our power. Prevents negative forces and
vibrations from affecting us. Good stone to use when
vulnerable, depleted, or lacking focus.

*Author's note: Be aware that if used long term or for several hours at a
time, it can bring forth a limiting or shut-off effect. Use only as
needed.*

PYRITE: "Money stone." Believed to attract money energies.
Brings clarity and sharper perception; shields us from
negativity. Enhances memory and decision making. Good
for periods after sickness. Has energizing properties and
aids in combatting fatigue and lethargy. Supports
respiratory function.

RHODONITE: Opens us to love and matters of the heart.
Supports forgiveness and unconditional love. Centering
and healing. Guides and redirects us to our true self and
the essence of the Universe. Helps reduce anxiety, anger,
and fear.

ROSE QUARTZ: "Love stone." Supports feelings of self-worth
and honoring the self. Heals emotional scars. Supports
relationships, love, and harmony. Calming. Excellent to
meditate with.

*Author's note: Hundreds of women and men have asked me to use this
stone to help them open their inner blockages with love. It is a true
opener for our emotional life and brings clarity to how we connect to
relationships. Also helps foster honesty in relationship.*

RUBY: A truly energizing and empowering stone that helps us to honor the self and our self-worth, and to feel vitality, renewal, and security. Reduces grief, brings resolve, promotes healing, generosity, spirituality, and courage. Wards off negative energies. Supports our sexual being, blood circulation, and the healing of infections.

SODALITE: Sharpens the mind; helps us to think with improved clarity and perception. Quiets inner chatter. Brings forth honesty, truth, wisdom, and a stabilizing vibration. Supports us in times of stress or ill health.

SNOW QUARTZ (SNOW STONE OR WHITE QUARTZ): Calming, restorative. Aids and supports us in balancing our feelings.

Author's note: I have used this stone—along with the girasol crystal—with great results to balance and bring forth the light of being and its joy.

TIGER'S EYE: Enhances courage and confidence. Supports movement. Opens up our energy field and brings clarity to taking action.

Author's note: I have found this stone very effective in helping us to "spring forth." I recommend starting with just a few minutes a day and see how your body reacts.

TOPAZ: "Stone of strength." Helps us discover, restore, and ease into our personal power. Lifts depression and negative patterns of thought. Strengthens the mental and emotional spheres.

Author's note: A truly powerful stone. Excellent for when we feel depleted of all energies. Use lightly at first since this is such a powerful stone.

TOURMALINE: Supports the alignment of the spiritual, physical, emotional, and mental. Connects us to the planet and all life energies. Guides us to find our placement in God's Creation. Releases self limitations and aids in awareness. A charged stone that wards off negative vibrations and pollutants in the environment.

TURQUOISE: "Stone of higher self." Protective, healing. Connects us to the higher realm and enhances our essence. Holy stone, promotes harmony.

ZOISITE: A slower-activating stone. Supports in creativity and honoring the self. Helps us to embrace our uniqueness. Good for warding off lethargy and detoxifying.

RECOMMENDED BOOKS ON STONE HEALING

Crystal Healing by Simon and Sue Lilly

The Healing Crystal First Aid Manual by Michael Gienger

The Crystal Bible by Judy Hall

RECOMMENDED WEBSITES ON STONE HEALING

crystal-cure.com

crystalvaults.com

crystalearthspirit.com

gemstonemeanings.us

crystalsandjewelry.com

acknowledgments

They say it takes a village to raise a child; I would also say it takes a team to champion the author to the finish line.

First and foremost, I would like to acknowledge my precious sister and dedicated editor, Minoo Rahbar, without whom this book would be sitting in a pile of my endless writings and would have never found its wings. Her precision, devotion, and belief in this little prayer book were beyond my expectations. I truly believe she was the only one who could honor my voice through the countless hours of editing, day after day, questioning me when I had deterred from the path of truth. She was the firm, yet tender, hand of an angel. For your seven-year labor of love, for your unwavering dedication to bring this book to fruition, and for helping me give this book wings, I am humbled, thankful, and speechless. Namaste.

To my beloved husband and soul-partner, Rama, for his love, caring, support, and unshakable belief in me throughout the years . . . you are my home, a gift from God upon my heart and life.

A most heartfelt gratitude to Lauren Sebastian for her grace, fortitude, patience, and her magical illustrations. Thank you for hearing and honoring my voice, and channeling it through your beautiful art. I could not imagine any other . . .

To my support team: Bobby Rock, for his guidance, tireless work, precision, and patience; Jackson Galaxy for his intuitive input, keen powers of observation, and for always cheering me on. Thank you both for your unwavering support and for guiding me through the haze. I am humbled.

This book would have been left in the hallways of my mind if it was not for the beautiful Jennifer Aniston, who on a full moon night, seven years ago, suggested that "the world needed to hear these prayers." For your generosity of heart, love, and support, I am eternally grateful.

To Dr. Michael Beckwith, Diane Lane, Billy Dee Williams, Courtney Cox, Sheryl Crow, Gisele Bundchen, Randolph Duke, and Hitesh Mehta: I am deeply humbled that you received the passages of this book with such generosity of spirit.

To Jane Dystel of Dystel & Goderich, for her belief in this book from the start, and for her constant support, unshakable belief, patience, and tenacity. To Miriam Goderich for her generous support and patience. A heartfelt thank-you to you both for guiding me on this new path.

To Sara Carder and the dedicated team at Tarcher/Penguin, including Joanna Ng, Brianna Yamashita, Kelli Daniels, Julianna Wilson, and Jessica Kaye, for their belief, efforts, and support in bringing forth this book of prayers to the world. Namaste.

To my beloved family, who was always there for me (despite being inconvenienced by my many months of writing in isolation). To Mahnaz for her unwavering love and support; Massoud for his continuous encouragement through the years; Jazz and Keyon, who make me want to be better; and my beloved Maman, for her undying love and devotion, and her poetic genes! I am grateful for you . . . you are each my heart.

To my many dear friends, extended family, students, and clients: thank you for your support and love, and for being part of the tapestry of my life. And my special gratitude to my dear friends Aida and Amira, for your help and continuous belief in me throughout the seven-year-long journey. I treasure you you all.

To my angels: Kristin Hahn, Mandy Ingber, Anita Rehker, Robin Le Measurer, Susie Mandel, and Liesl Taylor. You have graced me with your generosity of spirit and have been a reminder to me that even when *I* am not looking, God is.

To Monk Lawrence Freeman, Shahrooz Ash, and Gurutej Kaur Khalsa for the "word" (mantra).

To Chris Selak, Aleen Keshishian, Jeffrey Silberman, Yatrika Shah-Raiis, Carolyn McGuinness, Safoura Morovati, Melissa Stevens, Sophia Yen, and Janet Sode for their support and for graciously —and without pause—gifting me in this endeavor.

My heartfelt gratitude to those who have sat with me in various corners of the world in prayer, chanting the name of the Divine. You have fueled me with the energy to see this book through.

In deep gratitude and humility, I bow to the spirit world, who throughout the years of my channeling, has taught me more about love and God than I could have ever imagined. Thank you for choosing me to come through, and for teaching me that spirit never dies and is always our guiding light.

To the spirits of my dearest Mamina, Baba Mahmood, Daei Jahan, Nane Jooni; Ali, Saloumeh (for butterflies!), Sandra, Bruce, and my precious Zorba: I honor you always and you are each a part of me.

To my loving, dearest Khale Fakhri, and my precious Baba—I

know you were with me during countless nights of prayer, and are a joy within my being, my guiding lights.

And finally, to my Beloved, my Khoda—I am humbled by the hand of fate, and am eternally grateful to You for granting me with the strength and fortitude to see this through to the end with the support, guidance, and love of so many. You have driven this project, and I have learned to truly surrender to Your will. My journey with You is endless, loving, and full of awakening. I kneel to Your grace, eternally grateful, as I always sit at Your doorstep . . . Shokran.

If you enjoyed this book, visit

www.tarcherbooks.com

and sign up for Tarcher's e-newsletter to receive
special offers, giveaway promotions, and
information on hot upcoming releases.

TARCHER
PENGUIN

Great Lives Begin with Great Ideas

Connect with the Tarcher Community

• • •

Stay in touch with favorite authors!
Enter weekly contests!
Read exclusive excerpts!
Voice your opinions!

Follow us

 Tarcher Books

@TarcherBooks

If you would like to place a bulk order
of this book, call 1-800-847-5515.

also from tarcher

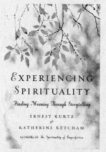

"A rich, thoughtful, and engaging collection of stories, anecdotes, quotations, and thoughts on all kinds of subjects that connect to spirituality from two people who understand spirituality better than anyone. Wonderful!"

—Susan Cheever

978-0-399-17512-1 · $16.95

"This book, both practical and profound, is a wonderful demonstration of just how to bring patience and a new way of being right into our daily lives. It is filled with insight, warmth, and compassion."

—Sharon Salzberg, author of *Real Happiness* and *Lovingkindness*

978-1-58542-900-4 · $14.95

"As founder and guiding teacher of the Community Meditation Center in New York, Allan Lokos has an arsenal of tools for coping with stressful situations."

—Rachel Lee Harris, *New York Times*

978-1-58542-781-9 · $13.95

DISCARD

APR - - 2016
348 1991